GUITAR-1

JOHN SEBASTIAN GASKIN

Beginning: Guitar - Music Theory - Sight Reading

Copyright © 2016 by John Sebastian Gaskin

All rights reserved. No part of this book may be reproduced or transmitted in any form without permission in writing from the publisher, including public performance for profit.

Jo-Kin Music, Trinidad and Tobago
jokinmusic@gmail.com

ISBN: 978-976-95914-2-4

Table Of Contents

0 - Introduction   *-1*

1 - The Guitar   *-2*

2 - The Positions   *-6*

3 - Four Rules   *-8*

4 - The Student   *-10*

5 - The Fretboard   *-12*

6 - Music Theory 101   *-14*

7 - Rhythmic Training 101   *-22*

8 - Fretboard Exercises 101   *-26*

9 - Sight Reading 101   *-32*

10 - Chords 101   *-34*

11 - Chord Exercises 101   *-38*

12 - Fretboard Exercises 102   *-42*

13 - Chords 102   *-46*

14 - Chord Exercises 102   *-50*

15 - Songs   *-54*

16 - References   *-i*

Dedicated To My Grand Boo-Boos.

"You are my Light, my Joy, my Hope"

0 - Introduction

"The Guitar belongs to the String Instrument family; along with the Harp, Violin, Cello, Sitar, Banjo, Zither, Lute, Cuatro and Mandolin."

The **Guitar** as we know it today was developed in the 1500's. Earlier string instruments began with one string, leading to ten and more strings on some of the instruments of today. The guitar has gone from being just an acoustic instrument to one that is also amplified with modern technology and electronics.

The guitar has also evolved with the many styles of music created through the years; Classical, Jazz, Rock, Country, Blues, to name a few. The guitar has remained popular over the years and the influences of past guitar players are a major reason why, players such as; Wes Montgomery, Joe Pass, Les Paul, Jimi Hendrix, B. B. King, Albert King, Andres Segovia, Carlos Santana, Julian Bream and others.

Guitar students have a choice of learning many styles of music on the guitar. However, there is no end to the learning of the guitar or music. Dedication to your craft is key to being a better musician. This book is all about learning to play the guitar. Do not be dismayed, practice slowly and often, and have *fun*. We all started out knowing absolutely nothing and sounding awful.

In this book the student will not only learn the guitar but also music theory and sight reading, while learning to play with the pick and fingerstyle.

1 - The Guitar

The Guitar is a string instrument. There are multiple varieties and combinations of acoustic and electric guitars.

Acoustic Guitars (Fig.1) are hollow body guitars that do not employ the use of any electronics to amplify their sound. They usually have a round sound hole on the guitar's front. They can have either nylon or metal strings for the top three strings. In some of the latest designs, there are multiple sound holes and shapes other than round. Acoustic guitars generate the sound through the sound hole. When a string is played, the sound vibrates in the hollow body of the instrument. It is amplified naturally and sent out through the sound hole.

Electric Guitars (Fig.2) have solid bodies with metal strings. Electric guitars use magnetic coils (pick-ups) to generate sound. When the string is played (plucked), the magnetic coil picks up the vibration of the string and converts it to electrical energy, which is converted to sound through the use of an amplifier. The more the string vibrates the higher the pitch of the sound produced. Thinner strings vibrate more than thicker ones.

Acoustic-Electric Guitars have a combination of sound holes and electronics with a hollow body.

"The Guitar is a subjective instrument and 'one size does not fit all'. Tone, feel and size are important features in choosing a guitar."

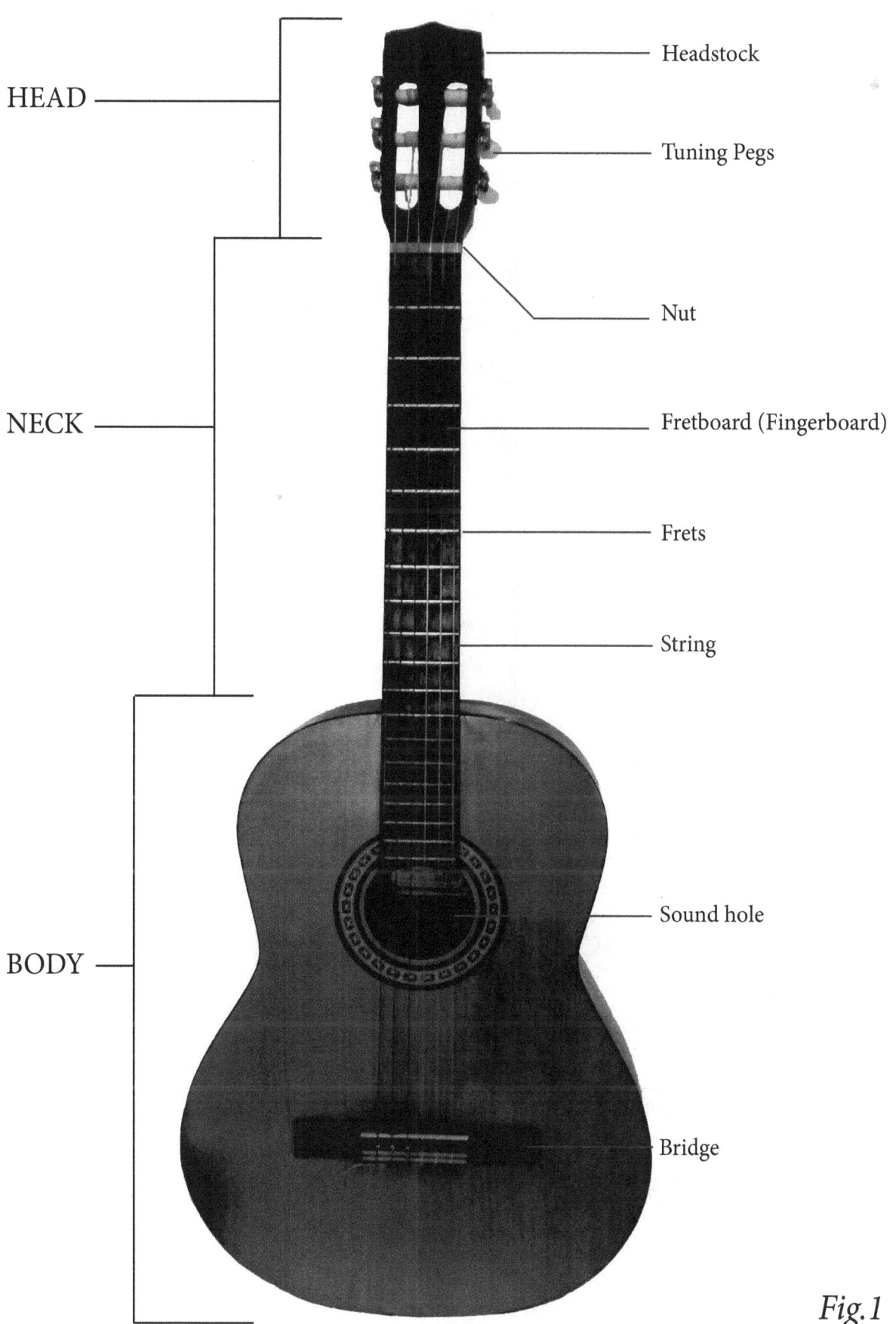

Fig.1

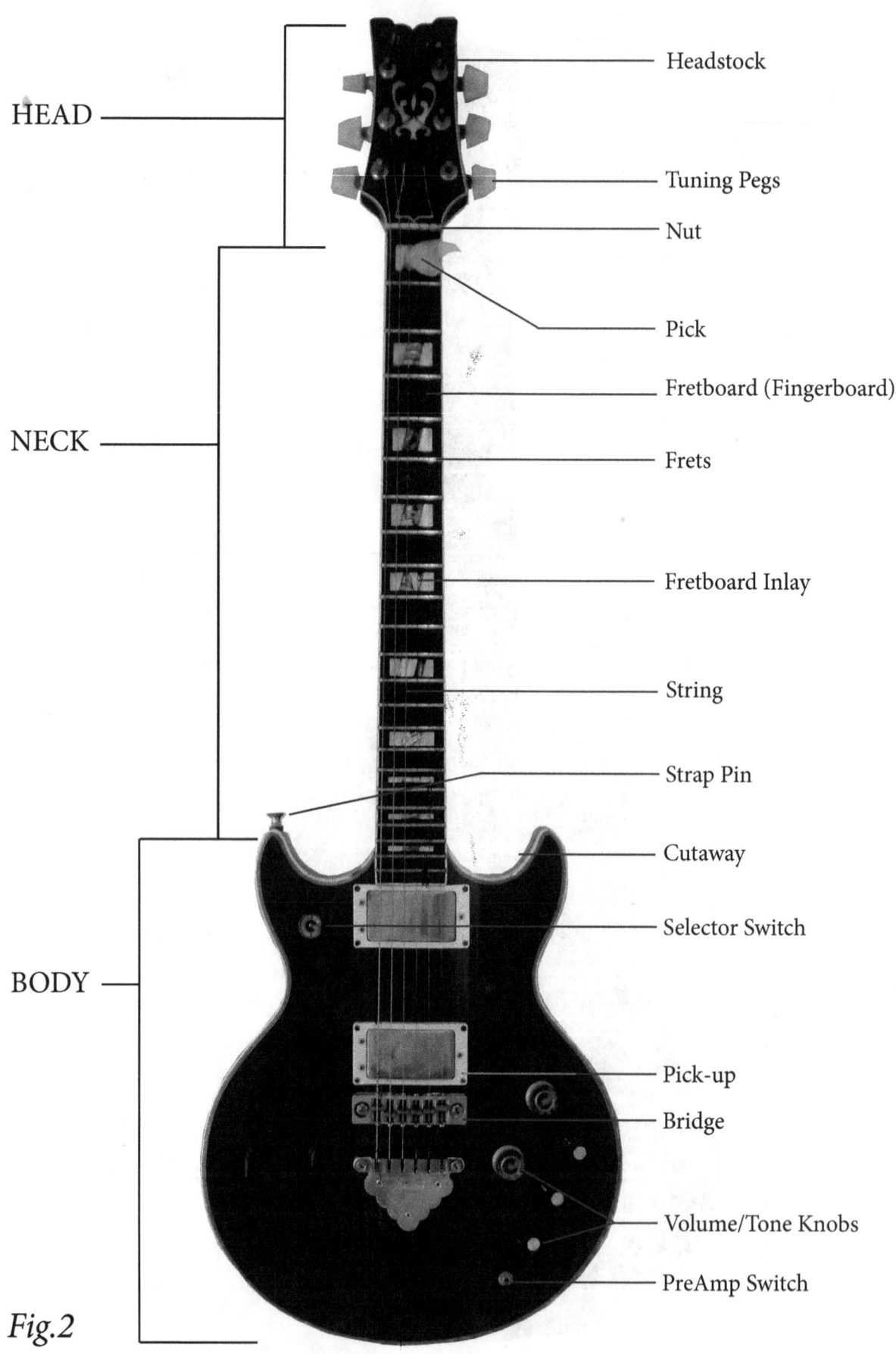

Fig.2

The Guitar has three major sections; the Head, the Neck and the Body (Fig.1 and 2).

"The Parts of an Acoustic Guitar are basically the same. The Parts of an Electric Guitar may vary based on style and use."

Bridge - The element where the bottom end of the strings are raised to clear the fretboard.

Fretboard - The wooden face of the neck that holds the frets and where the fingers press the strings.

Frets - The metal strips across the fretboard dividing the fretboard, enabling different pitches on each string.

Headstock - The top of the guitar that holds the tuning pegs (machine heads).

Nut - The element between the head and neck where the strings pass.

Output Jack - The hole on the body that allows the guitar cable (jack) to be inserted.

Pick-up - Magnetic coils below the strings on the body that creates electrical energy as the strings vibrate.

Selector Switch - The switch that allows different pickups to be selected.

Sound Hole - The hole in the face of the guitar that projects sound.

Strap Pin - The pins on the edges for guitar straps to be anchored.

Tuning Pegs - The machinery holding the top of the strings and wound for proper tuning.

Volume/Tone Knobs - Knobs on an electric guitar that are used for volume and various guitar tones.

2 - The Positions

The Position of the guitar, while seated, for practice or performance will be decided on according to the style of music to be learnt. The student should be comfortable in the position chosen. The waist of the guitar is usually placed on the left leg for classical style (Fig.3), and a footstool is most times used when playing classical music in a sitting position. Other times an apparatus to raise the guitar into position from the lap is used, one type is called the **A-Frame**. For other styles of music in the sitting position, the waist of the guitar sits on the right leg (Fig.4).

Fig.3 *Fig.4*

"The position of the guitar and performer is determined by the style of music to be performed, guitarist preference and style of guitar."

With the guitar on the right leg, the student should sit with both thighs parallel to the floor. This helps to keep the guitar and student steady. The guitar should be placed just in front of the student's body and angled up from the body of the guitar to the head, Figs.3 and Fig.4. The body of the guitar should be tilted backward *slightly* and the performer leaning forward to see the front of the guitar. The left arm and hand should be angled up towards the neck and the fingers bent towards the fretboard in what I call the 'crab' position. The thumb of the left hand should be vertical on the back of the neck and the pressure point just around the middle of the arch of the neck.

The right arm should be anchored at the elbow on the top of the guitar at the middle of the base arch, Fig.3 and Fig.4. The right hand should fall and be positioned just in front of the sound hole. To diminish the sound coming from the sound hole the hand should be positioned directly in front of the sound hole. To allow more sound out of the sound hole the hand should be placed away from the sound hole closer to the bridge.

The body of the student performer should be upright at all times. The student's head and neck would be bent slightly forward to view the fretboard and strings. Good posture is important for all performers and their endurance in pursuit of proper guitar playing. Classical guitarists perform in a sitting position while other performers with other musical styles play either sitting or standing.

3 - Four Rules

Rule #1 - Always tune your guitar (Fig.6) before every practice. This will ensure proper tuning every time. You, the student, will also learn to relate the note sounded to the name of the note. Students should hum each note of the open string as they tune. This will be the beginning of the student's ear training.

Rule #2 - Always use a metronome (Fig.5) when practicing. This will ensure that you, the student, develop proper timing. Timing is very important in music. It is truly one of its key components. The metronome should always be set to a slow beat when first starting an exercise. Always start practice with the metronome set at 40 beats per minute.

Rule #3 - Practice all exercises slowly. This is to ensure proper and effective fingering for each exercise. The student can increase speed gradually as he/she becomes adept to the exercises. "It is not about how fast you can play but how well you can play."

Rule #4 - Practice often, one hour a day minimum, including light finger stretches. "Constant practice helps the fingers remember." It is not about just having mental recall of the exercises or songs, but the fingers get accustomed to the movements along the fretboard. The muscles of the fingers get a workout, which helps them to remember and makes fingering easier.

"It is not about how fast you can play, but how well you can play. It takes a lot of concentration to play slowly and keep proper timing."

Binding - The decoration around the body of the guitar.

Bridge Pins - The pin like elements that holds down the ball end of the strings on the bridge.

Fingerboard - This is the fretboard without the metal frets, fretless.

Fingering - The use of the fingers on either hand to play the guitar.

Metronome - A device which creates sounds or light pulses with a specifically set timing. It could be sped up or slowed down.

Open Strings - Strings played without the left hand fingers pressing the strings at any fret.

Pick - A small plastic, metallic or synthetic triangular item used to pluck the strings to play the guitar.

Rosette - The decoration around the round sound hole on acoustic guitars, mainly classical guitars.

Tuner - A device used to tune instruments.

Tuning - The process of creating the correct pitches for the open strings by turning the tuning pegs.

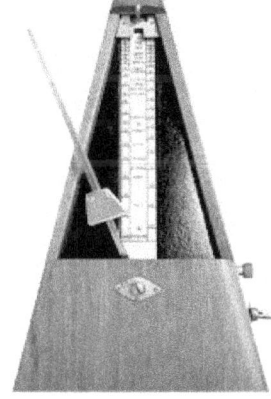

Fig.5 - Metronomes

Fig.6 - Tuners

4 - The Student

In the past students of guitar only learnt to play the guitar in whatever style the teacher knew, or as the student wanted. Music theory was basically non-existent, but the student developed his/her ear. It is very important today for the student to learn music theory, sight reading and develop their ear as they learn to play the guitar. This is important if one is to take this instrument seriously and wants to earn a livelihood from playing the guitar.

The student must learn his instrument. The student must learn each part of his guitar physically (Fig.1 and Fig.2). The student must learn each part of his guitar musically, every note on every fret (Fig.7). This last item will take some time but students should be diligent in this pursuit. This will help the student in their sight reading, scales and chord locations on the fretboard.

The student should understand each assignment clearly and must practice each assignment diligently before proceeding to the next. The student should be comfortable and relaxed while attempting the exercises. This will help with concentration. This book will take the student through all elements of music to ensure the student is proficient in guitar playing and theory, and versed to communicate with other musicians, no matter what instruments they may play.

"The performer can use a pick (plectrum), or fingers (fingerstyle also called finger picking) to play the guitar with the right hand."

> "A good student is one who is willing to learn, practice what they have learnt so that they can improve their status."

For beginning students, I recommend learning first on a nylon string guitar. Steel strings, especially the thinner strings, will cut and damage delicate fingers and quickly discourage students from progressing. The student should be comfortable in both body position and understanding of the work being taught throughout this book.

The student should always set the metronome at 40 beats per minute to start practicing each exercise, and gradually increase the tempo as playing improves. As stated earlier, it is very important for the student to practice slowly.

A reminder to the student, tune the guitar before each practice session. While tuning the student should hum the notes of the open string being tuned. This will reinforce the notes into the memory of the students, and thus ear training begins.

It is not important which tuner or metronome a student buys and uses. They all do the same things. There are even combinations of tuner and metronome. For the beginning student it is recommended not to buy expensive devices. At this stage of learning there is no benefit to having the expensive gadgets. A student should not abuse their equipment. No matter how big or small, respect your instrument. Always clean your equipment after use. This will ensure longer life of the equipment and a better performance every time.

5 - The Fretboard

The **Fretboard**, also called the fingerboard, (Fig.7) shows all the notes to be played on the guitar. The notes shown in letter form above the nut -E-A-D-G-B-E- are the notes of the open strings, tuned. In this book we will be using this standard, most common tuning. There are other types of tuning but they will not be addressed in this book. The numbers above, 6 (thickest) to 1 (thinnest), refers to the string numbering system.

The frets divide the fretboard to accurately produce required pitches from each string. When a string is 'played', it is the action of the finger pressing a string onto the fretboard just behind a specified 'fret'. This 'fret' and the corresponding section of the fretboard preceding it are given the same reference number. So the student may be asked to "play the third string at the fifth fret." In Fig.7 we see that the third string (G string) at the fifth fret produces the pitch 'C'.

Middle 'C' on the guitar occurs in different places (fret locations) and on different strings, as do many other notes. The guitar is like other string instruments in this regard. This opens up a vast array of possibilities with chords and melodies. Notes on the fifth fret are the same as the next open string, except for the third string. From one fret to the adjacent fret gives a chromatic half step interval, every two frets give an interval of a whole step, F-G (Fig.7). At the twelfth fret

"The fretboard comes in several wood options; Ebony, Rosewood and Maple. The different woods give different tones and feel to the performer."

the notes on the strings across the fretboard are the same as the notes of the strings played 'open'. As such, the notes on the thirteenth fret are the same as those on the first fret and so on, the fretboard repeats.

"The Fretboard of the guitar is set up chromatically. Plucking a string from one fret to an adjacent fret creates a half step interval."

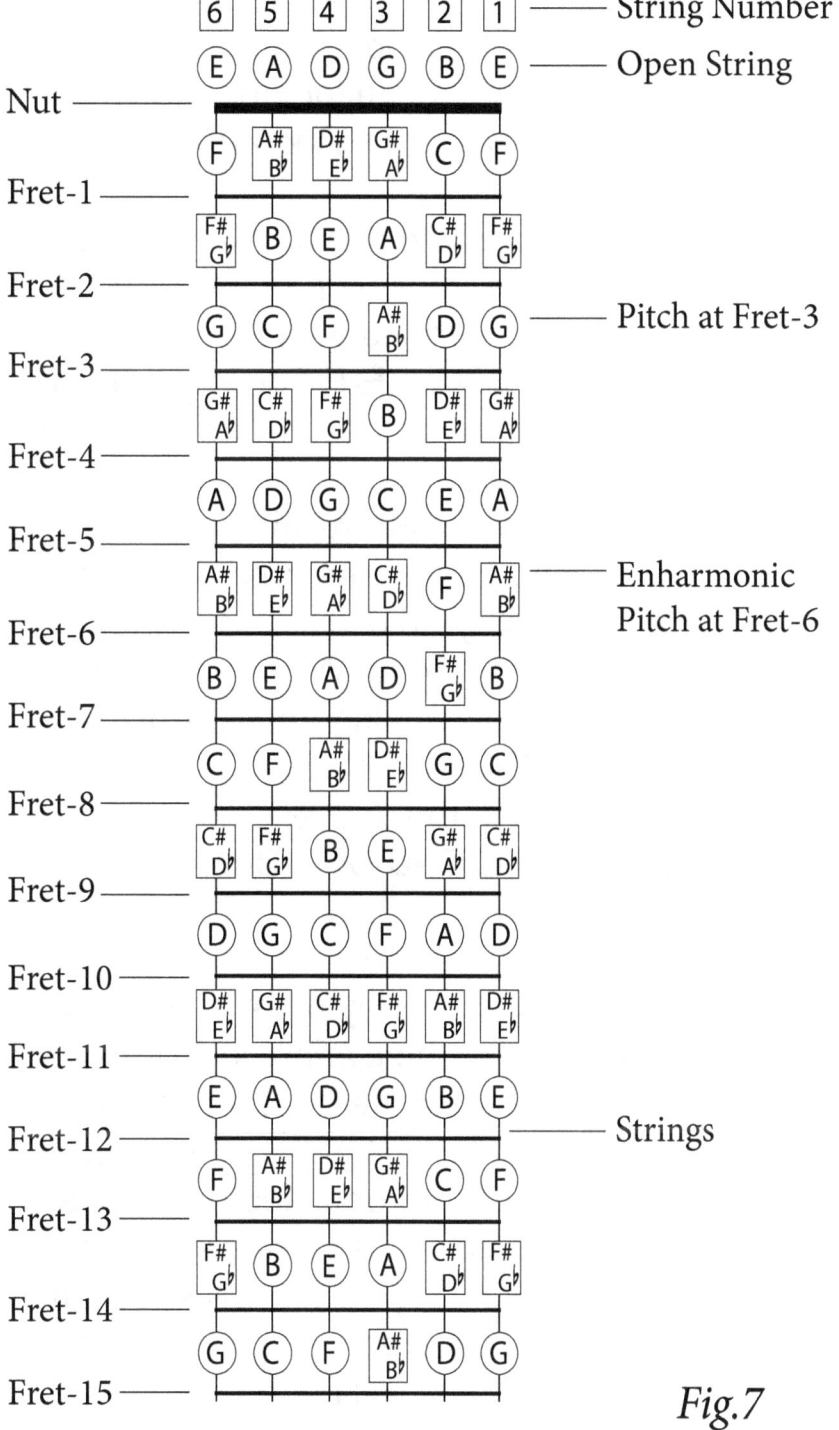

Fig.7

6 - Music Theory 101

There are seven natural pitches in music: **A-B-C-D-E-F-G**. These pitches repeat themselves every eight pitch creating higher or lower octaves. This can be easily seen on a piano keyboard but not easily on the guitar. These pitches, on the guitar, are shown in circles in the Fretboard section (Fig.7).

The **Chromatic Scale** has all twelve musical pitches. They are the seven mentioned above plus five intermediary pitches: A-**A#(B♭)**-B-C-**C#(D♭)**-D-**D#(E♭)**-E-F-**F#(G♭)**-G-**G#(A♭)**-A. All intermediary pitches have two names, A# (A-sharp) is also called B♭ (B-flat). They are referred to as **Enharmonic**. There are no sharps or flats between the notes B-C and E-F. However, they do occur. We will touch on them as we go along. When pitches are indicated in the ascending order **Sharps** are used: A-A#-B-C-C#-D-D#-E-F-F#-G-G#-A. When indicated in the descending order **Flats** are used: E-E♭-D-D♭-C-B-B♭-A-A♭-G-G♭-F-E.

"Do not use sharps and flats together. This will create confusion when working out the key of a composition and chord qualities."

Many instruments employ other keys, as with the B♭ trumpet and the clarinet in A. Music for the guitar is written in the **Treble Clef** and in the key 'Concert C'. The guitar is referred to as the treble guitar, as opposed to the bass guitar. The treble clef is also referred to as the 'G' clef or sign (Fig.8). We will show other clef signs in this book as we teach certain musical features. We will not be teaching the many musical clef signs in this book.

"Enharmonic tones carry two names such as A# and B♭, but have the same sound (frequency and pitch)."

Accidentals - Signs indicating whether notes are 'sharp-(#)', 'flat-(♭)' or 'natural-(♮)' in pitch.

Chord - Several notes played together for accompaniment, as soloist or group.

Chromatic - Half step intervals between notes. B-C-C#-D-D#-E-F.

Clef - The sign indicating the range in which musical notes occur and indicative of the musical tuning of the instrument.

Harmony - When more than one note is played at the same time.

Key - The note scale used in a composition.

Measure - Section of the staff between the vertical bar lines.

Melody - When one note is played after the other respective of pitch.

Note - The symbol on the musical staff, on the line or in a space indicating pitch.

Octave - Eight musical notes, the seven musical notes and the root repeated at the eight scale tone.

Pitch - The frequency of a note, the faster the frequency the higher the pitch.

Rests - The symbol on the musical staff indicating when not to play (rest).

Scale - A series of notes played in order of ascending or descending starting and ending on the key note.

Staff - The five horizontal lines creating a musical score (sheet music) where notes are placed.

Time Signature - The two numbers, one above the other, at the beginning of the staff after the clef sign.

There are different notes in music and they have their corresponding rest signs. The Whole note (o) represents four beats. Two Half notes (𝅗𝅥) equal one whole note. Two Quarter notes (♩) equal one half note. Two Eight notes (♪) equal one quarter note. Two Sixteenth notes (𝅘𝅥𝅯) equal one eight note (Fig.11 and Fig.12). The Quarter note is the most common beat in music.

The beat in an actual music score will be determined by the time signature. In 6/8 timing the eight note represents one beat in that musical composition. We will continue with timing and rhythm in the following section of Rhythmic Training. We will not be looking at thirty-second notes or rests in this book. For the student's information, two thirty-second notes or rests equal one sixteenth note or rest.

Rests have values similar to notes. There are Whole rests, Half rests, Quarter rests, Eight rests, Sixteenth rests (Fig.13). Think of rests as chances to catch your breadth.

The notes on the Treble Clef (Fig.10) start from '**Middle-C**' on the ledger line below the staff and goes above the staff. The notes on the guitar that fall above or below the staff will be written on or between ledger lines (Fig.9). The shaded notes in Fig.9 indicate the pitches of the open strings, Fig.7. The notes go up alphabetically, no skipping; C-D-E-F-G-A-B-C +. Reading from right to left and as such, bottom to top. The notes on the lines in the staff are E-G-B-D-F.

"The top number of the time signature indicates the number of notes in the measure. The bottom number indicates type of note."

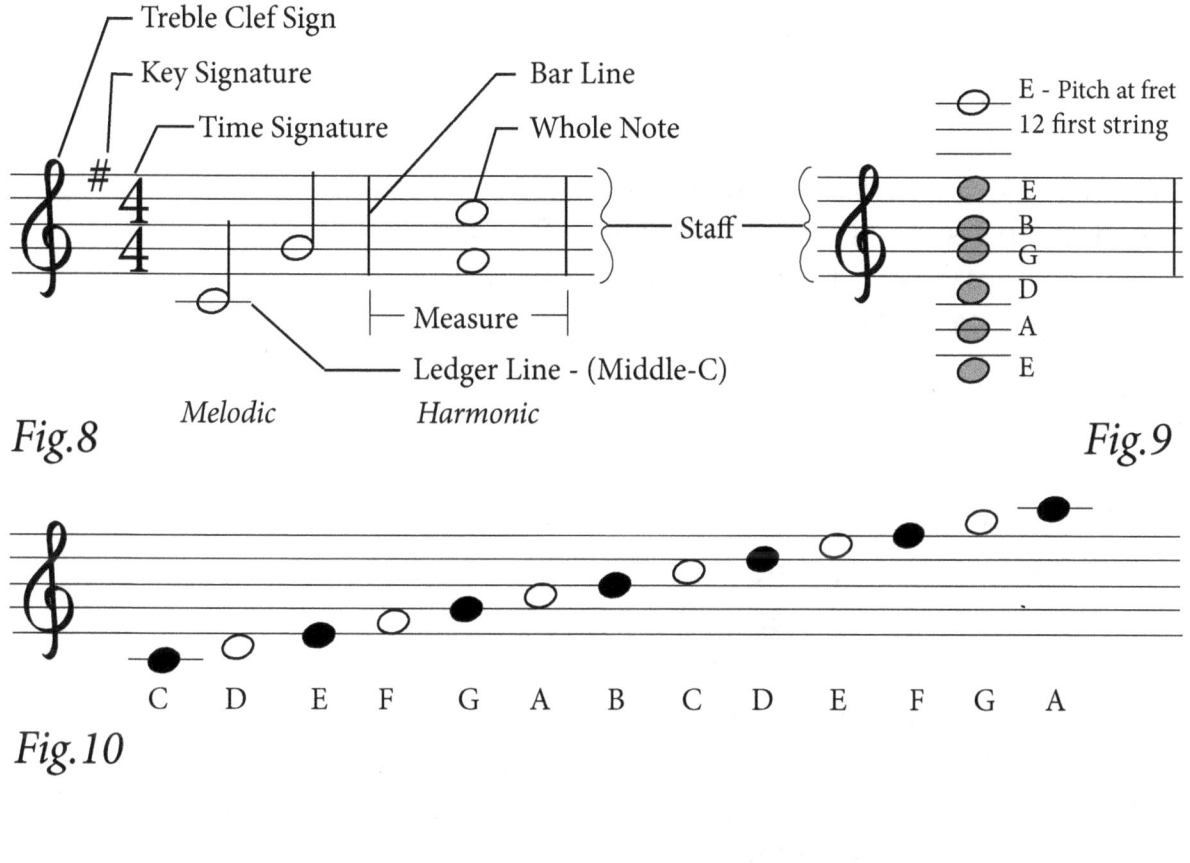

Fig.8   Fig.9

Fig.10

1 whole note = 2 half notes = 4 quarter notes = 8 eight notes

Fig.11

8 sixteenth notes = 4 eight notes = 2 quarter notes = 1 half note

Fig.12

The notes in the spaces are F-A-C-E. The notes on the line and those in the spaces skip alphabetically (Fig.10). Once you know where Middle-C is on the guitar you can find the other notes.

We mentioned earlier in this section that there are no sharps or flats between B-C and E-F. As mentioned, they do happen. If you look at the F# Major scale on the next page (Fig.14) you will see an E# note. The note cannot be called F as there is already an 'F' in the scale (F#). This can also be seen in the G♭ scale where C♭ occurs. The alphabet has to be followed and no doubling of letters can occur. The root notes in the scales with sharps, C-G-D-A-E-B-F#, have intervals of a 'perfect fifth' from note to note, and is referred to as the **Circle of Fifths**. The root notes in the scales with flats, C-F-B♭-E♭-A♭-D♭-G♭, have intervals of a 'perfect fourth' from note to note, and is referred to as the **Cycle of Fourths**.

An **Major Scale** is made up of eight pitches (notes) with intervals of five whole steps and two half steps (Fig.15). In Fig.14 you see some of the Major Scales in music, those with sharps and those with flats occurring. A Major Scale is also known as a **Diatonic** Scale, from the **Tonic.** Other scales have different intervals between notes and may not start on the Tonic, which differentiate each scale. Intervals are measured from first (root) pitch to every other pitch in the scale and are linked to the distance, whole step or half step (semi-tone), between each pitch.

"All notes and rests should be played and held for their required duration as written. Only when there are accents on the notes that their duration changes"

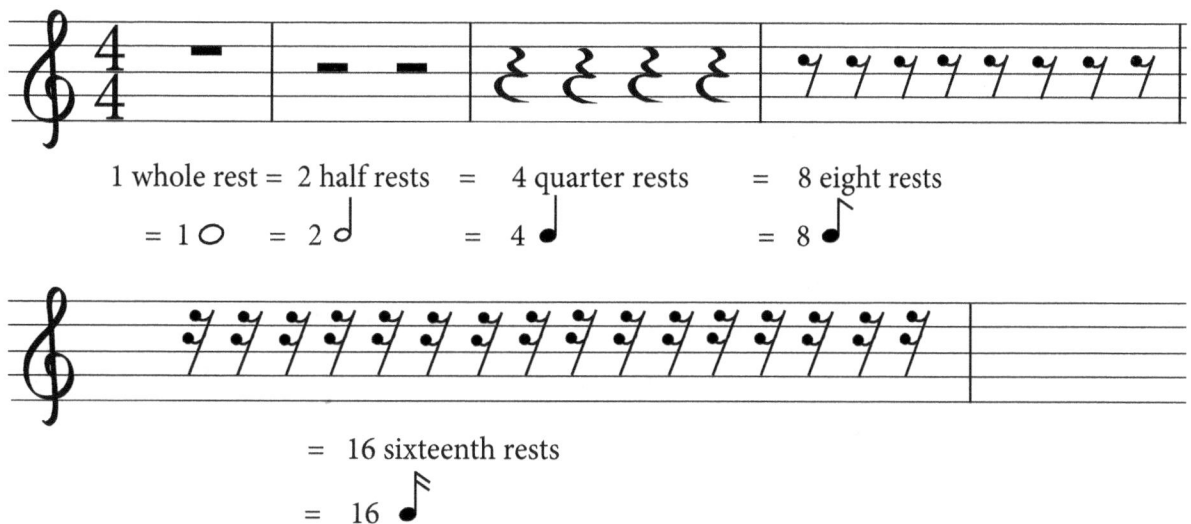

Fig.13

MAJOR SCALES:

Root	Sharps or Flats	Scale Notes
C	None	C-D-E-F-G-A-B-C
G	1 Sharp	G-A-B-C-D-E-F#-G
D	2 Sharps	D-E-F#-G-A-B-C#-D
A	3 Sharps	A-B-C#-D-E-F#-G#-A
E	4 Sharps	E-F#-G#-A-B-C#-D#-E
B	5 Sharps	B-C#-D#-E-F#-G#-A#-B
F#	6 Sharps	F#-G#-A#-B-C#-D#-E#-F#
F	1 Flat	F-G-A-B♭-C-D-E-F
B♭	2 Flats	B♭-C-D-E♭-F-G-A-B♭
E♭	3 Flats	E♭-F-G-A♭-B♭-C-D-E♭
A♭	4 Flats	A♭-B♭-C-D♭-E♭-F-G-A♭
D♭	5 Flats	D♭-E♭-F-G♭-A♭-B♭-C-D♭
G♭	6 Flats	G♭-A♭-B♭-C♭-D♭-E♭-F-G♭

Fig.14

As mentioned previously, from one fret on the guitar to an adjacent fret is a measurement (distance) of a semi-tone, or half step. Any distance two frets away creates a whole step measurement (F-G, B-C#). Fig.15 shows the distance between notes in the B♭ scale. In a Major scale the distance (measurement) between notes are listed as 'W-W-H-W-W-W-H' (W=whole steps and H=half steps or semi-tone).

The other intervals shown in Fig.15 are those from the root note to other notes in the scale. From B♭ (root) to C (2nd) is an interval of a Major Second (one whole step or two half steps). From B♭ to D (3rd) is an interval of a Major Third (two whole steps or four half steps). From B♭ to E♭ (4th) is an interval of a Perfect Fourth (two whole steps and a half step). B♭ to F (5th) is an interval of a Perfect Fifth (three whole steps and a half step). From B♭ to G (6th) is a Major Sixth (four whole steps and one half step). B♭ to A (7th) is an interval of a Major Seventh (Five whole steps and one half step). B♭ to B♭ (8th) is an interval of an Octave (Six whole steps, or broken down is five whole steps and two half steps). The same pitched note played twice is an interval called a Unison.

With this information anyone can build a major scale off of any note in music. This information will take time to understand and learn. So, practice, practice, practice. Go over parts of the lessons as you need to. Always remember two half steps (two semi-tones) are equal to one whole step.

"Chords (root, third and fifth) built from any diatonic note of a particular scale should always have notes from that particular scale. The root of the chord is the note the chord is built from, different from the scale root."

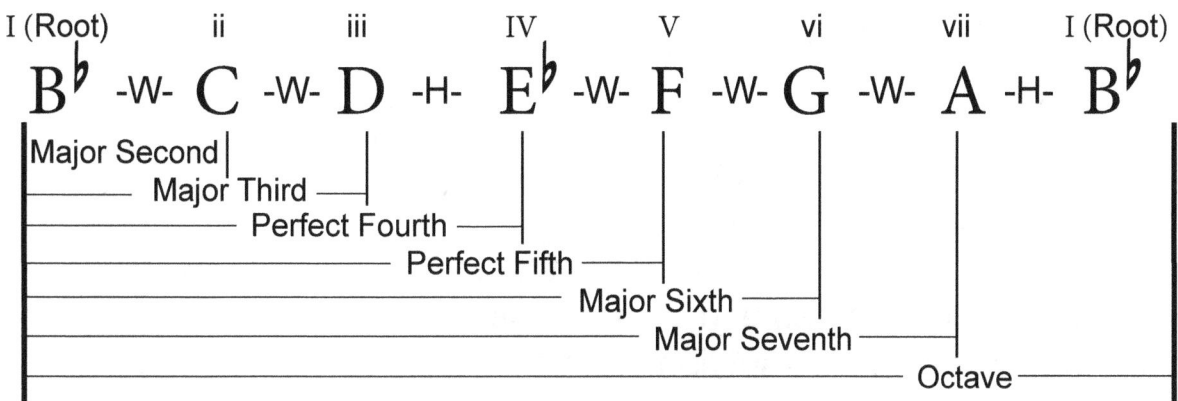

Fig.15

Arpeggio - Also called Broken Chord, is the playing of the notes of a chord in sequence, one after the other.

Bar Lines - Vertical lines on the musical staff separating measures.

Beat - The musical pulse of a composition.

Dotted Note - A Note with a Dot just after it adds half the value of that note back on to the note.

Interval - The musical reference to distance (measurement) between notes.

Inversion - A chord with different notes in the bass or lowest register, other than the root note.

Ledger Line - The short line above or below the staff where notes are shown.

Progression - A series of chords played one after the other.

Root - The note a scale or chord is built on.

Strum - Playing a number of strings at the same time.

Tie - The line connecting notes to each other that allows the duration of the first note to be added (tied) to the second note.

Triad - A chord with three notes.

7 - Rhythmic Training 101

Knowing the different musical notes, rests and their values are important to learning rhythm. Practice is the other important factor. We have learnt the notes and their values in the Music Theory 101 section. In this section we will not be concentrating much on the guitar. This section is about rhythm, so sounding the note and tapping the beat matching the metronome is to be performed.

In the exercises in this section we show the drum staff. There are no pitch values in this staff just note values. Here we are using 4/4 timing, four quarter notes per measure. Each quarter note is a beat. The student should set the metronome to 40 and count the beats slowly, 1-2-3-4, 1-2-3-4,1-2-3-4. All notes are sung or played for its required duration.

In Fig.16 the beat and quarter note are the same so the student should be sounding and counting 1-2-3-4, 1-2-3-4, 1-2-3-4, with the metronome. In Fig.17 two eight notes equal a quarter note beat. The student should be sounding 1-&-2-&-3-&-4-&, where the '&' is on the upbeat. In Fig.18 the half note equals two quarter note beats. The notes occur on the first and third beats and must be held for its duration, the full two beats. In Fig.19 the whole note equals four quarter note beats and should be held for the entire measure. In Fig.20 four sixteenth notes equal one quarter note beat. The student should sound the four notes in the space of each beat.

"I advise anyone who is learning to read music to get the book, 'Rhythmic Training' by Robert Starer. It is a great book."

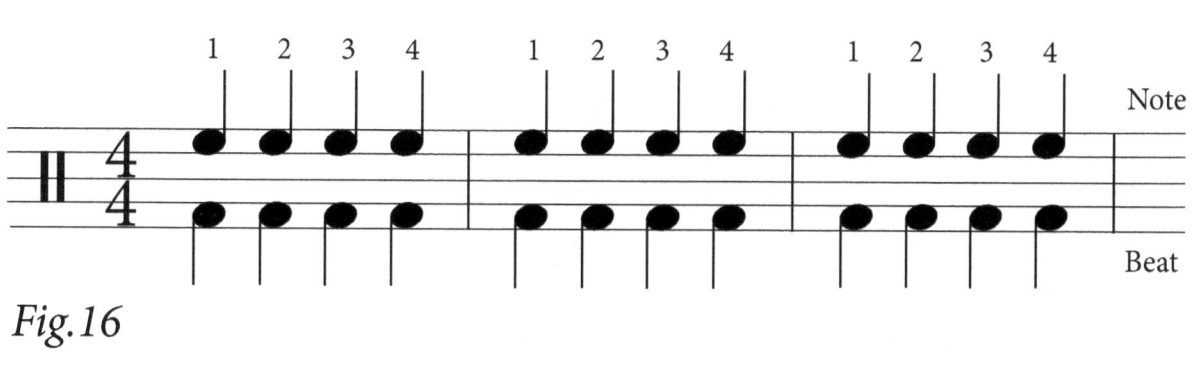

Fig.16

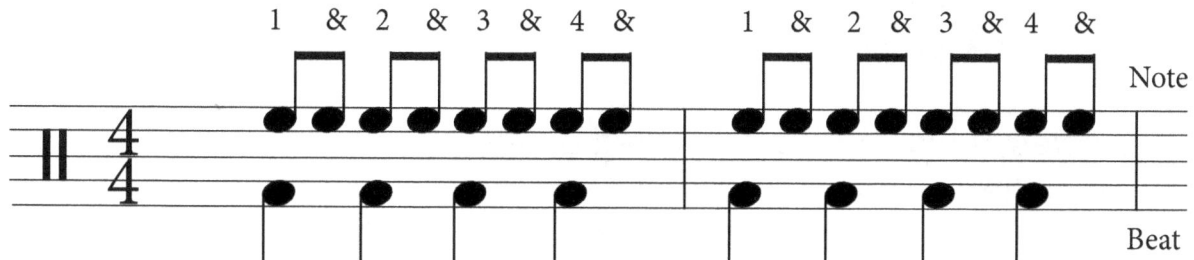

Fig.17

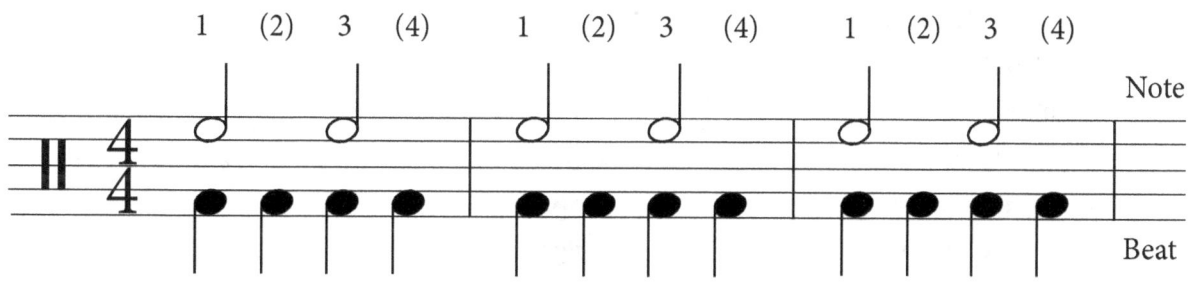

Fig.18

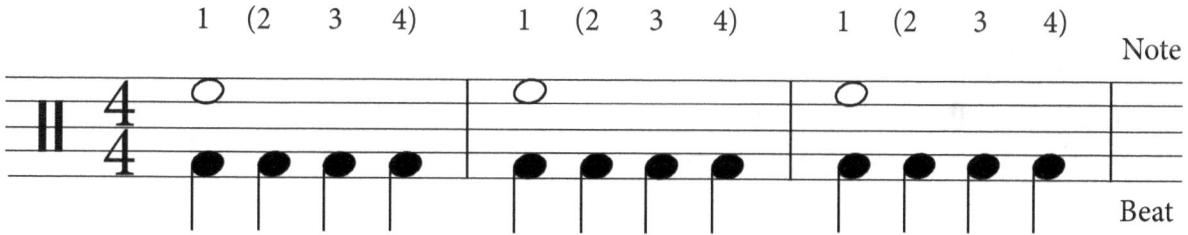

Fig.19

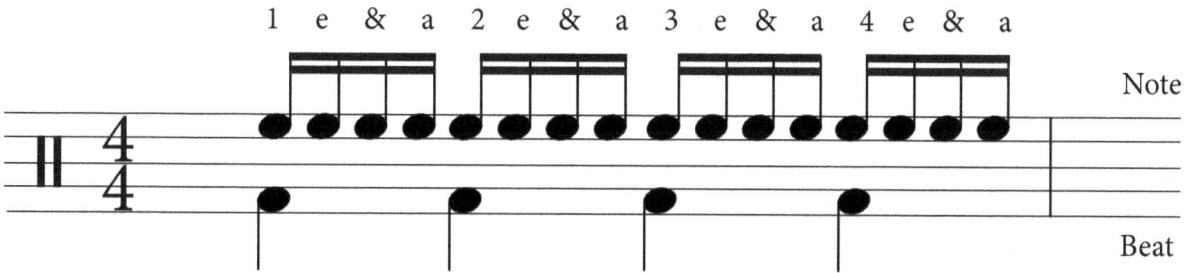

Fig.20

Practice each exercise until it is well understood and accomplished before moving to the next. In Fig.21 the notes are mixed to provide some challenge for you, the student. As always go slowly with the metronome on 40 beats per minute. Go back to the previous exercises if something poses an issue to play or follow properly.

The notes in Fig.21 may be played on the guitar. If the student is comfortable with the exercise then playing the notes using one single note on the guitar can be a plus. You will also be practicing your playing techniques, pressing the first string at the first fret with the index finger of the left hand. For fingerstyle playing the student shall pluck the notes with the index (i) and middle (m) fingers using alternating strokes. Playing with the pick the student shall play alternating down and up strokes. Go slowly. More will be discussed about fingering in the following Fretboard Exercises 01 section.

We have been told in the Music Theory 101 section about the dot after a note and the note 'tie'. In Fig.22 the exercise adds these values to the score making it even more challenging to the student. This exercise needs even more concentration, and practice, practice slowly. You should not be dismayed or despondent if it takes a while to master these exercises. Be patient and take your time. Good things will happen. Once the student can play these exercises clearly and efficiently, reading music will become that much easier.

"If possible sound the notes using a syllable like 'LA', while trying to tap the beat with your hand or feet. Again, practice slowly."

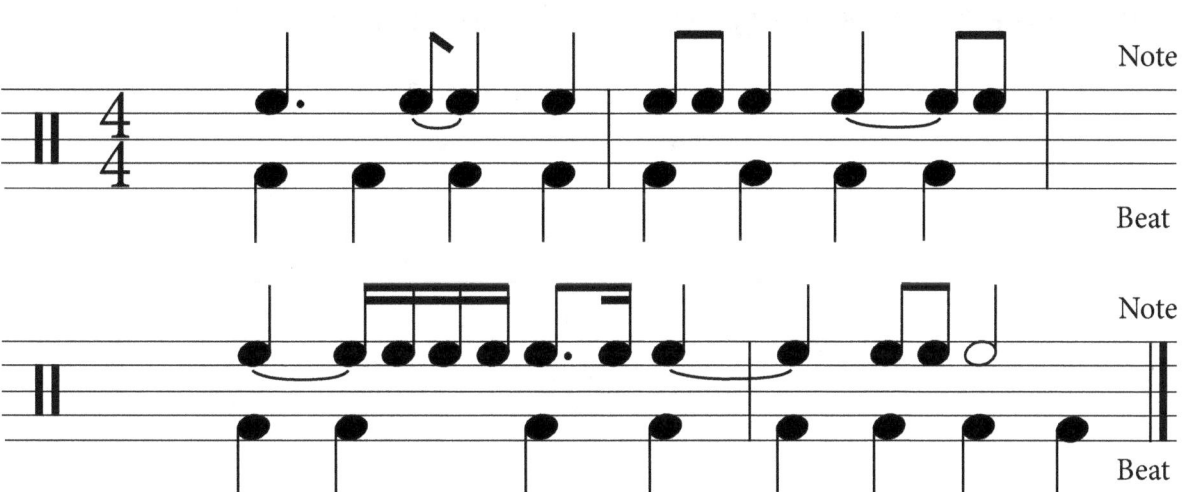

Fig.21

Fig.22

8 - Fretboard Exercises 101

Students will learn to play the guitar with both their fingers (fingerstyle), and the pick (plectrum). As a student progresses then a decision would be made to play with just the fingers and/or pick. This will be determined mainly by the style of music the student wants to concentrate on and be proficient at.

FINGERSTLYE:
Each finger has a designation in music. The right hand has a letter per finger, and the left has a number per finger, except the thumb (Fig.23). This tells the student which finger to play and where.
The left hand fingers press the strings at the frets to give specific pitches. The right hand fingers pluck the strings to give sound. The strings should be played with the fingertips of the right hand. There are others who are trained to play the strings with fingertips and nail. Nails on the left hand should be clipped low. Nails on the right hand should be in line with the fingertips and properly manicured. The thumb on the right hand is anchored on a string, pickup or side of the fretboard. The fingers of the right hand are pointed slightly towards the bridge of the guitar. The fingers will provide either a **Rest Stroke** or **Free Stroke**, and the student gets the next finger to be used into position and 'prepared' to play the next note. Left handed players shall use a reverse reading of the hands.

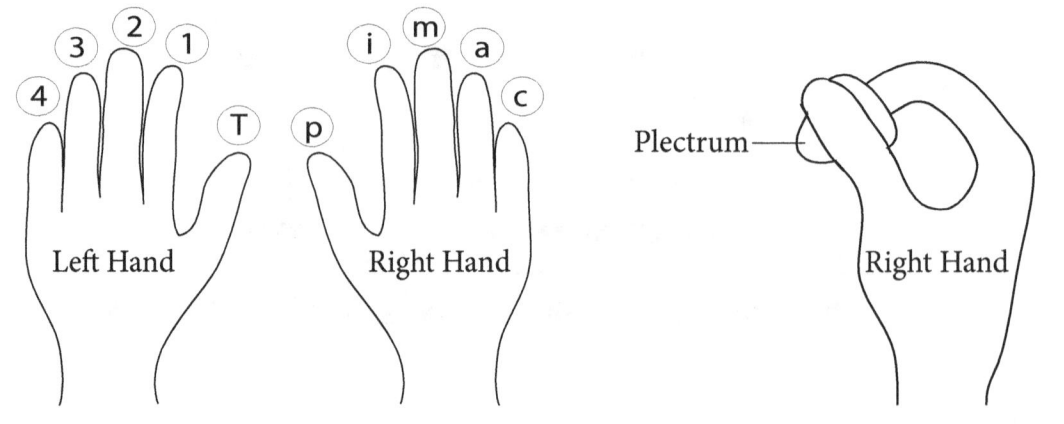

Fig.23   *Fig.24*

Free Stroke - The process of playing a string with a finger and not resting the finger on any string after playing.

Mute - To dampen, not sound, a string by slightly touching it with one of the left hand fingers, or right palm.

Rest Stroke - The process of playing a string with a finger and resting the finger on an adjacent string after playing.

PLECTRUM STYLE:

While fingerstyle is mainly used in classical and some folk music, the plectrum (pick) is used in just about every other style of music. The plectrum comes in many shapes, materials and thicknesses. The student will decide which pick he/she is comfortable with and the tone it produces. All picks no matter what size or shape have at least one point. This point is used to strike the strings. The pick is positioned on the index finger with the point in the direction the finger is pointed. The thumb is then positioned over the pick with the thumb pointed perpendicular to the index finger, creating a cross with the two fingers (Fig.24). How firmly you grip the pick will depend on your style and feel, which will create your own tone and voice on the guitar. The other fingers are to be in a closed position, out of the way of the strings. The picking hand is not to touch the guitar. The student shall use alternate upstroke (U) (V) and downstroke (D) (⊓) picking using the plectrum starting with the down stroke unless noted otherwise. All picking movement shall employ the wrist and not the elbow.

"The numbers on the fingers of the left hand represent the numbers and the placement of the fingers on the fretboard. See Fig.23, Fig.26A and Fig.27A."

HYBRID PICKING:
The art of using both plectrum and fingers to simultaneously or alternatively pluck the strings.

The following exercises are drills and must be diligently practiced. The exercises show alternate picking on each string, see the information above the staves. Tune the guitar and set the metronome to 40. Repeat until the exercises are played comfortably, smoothly and in time with the metronome. The notes should be even in rhythm, tone and volume when done correctly.

Exercise 1:
In Fig.25 the student shall pluck the open first string (E) until the notes are played comfortably in alternate pattern and with each stroke matching the beat of the metronome.

Exercise 2:
In Fig.26 and Fig.26A, the student shall press the first fret on the first string with the first finger and pluck the string four times; then press the second fret with the second finger and pluck four times; then press the third fret with the third finger and pluck four times; and finally, press the fourth fret with the fourth finger and pluck four times. In Fig.27 and Fig.27A, the student shall press the first fret on the second string with the first finger and pluck the string four times; then press the second fret with the second finger and pluck four times; then press the third fret with the third finger and pluck four times; and finally, press the fourth fret with the fourth finger and pluck four times. Then do the same on the third and fourth strings.

Exercise 3:
Play the notes in exercise 2 backwards, from the fourth fret going back to the first fret on each of the four strings starting on the first string.

Exercise 4:
Play the notes in exercise 2, from the fourth string down to the first string, and from the first fret to the fourth fret on all four strings.

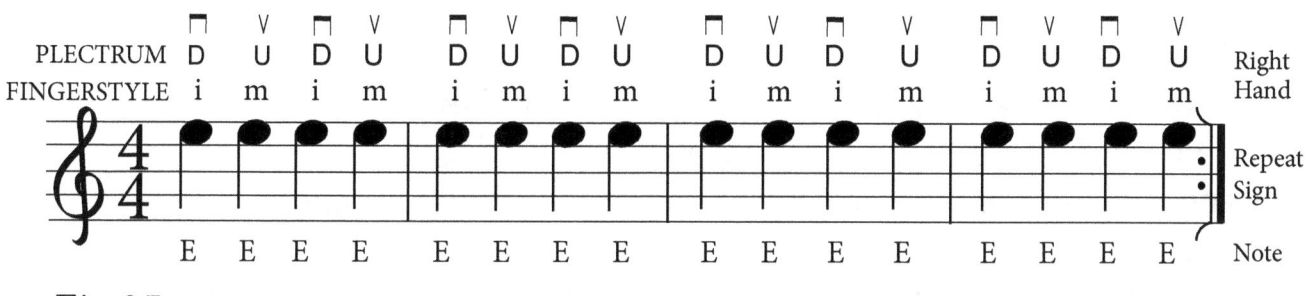

Fig.25

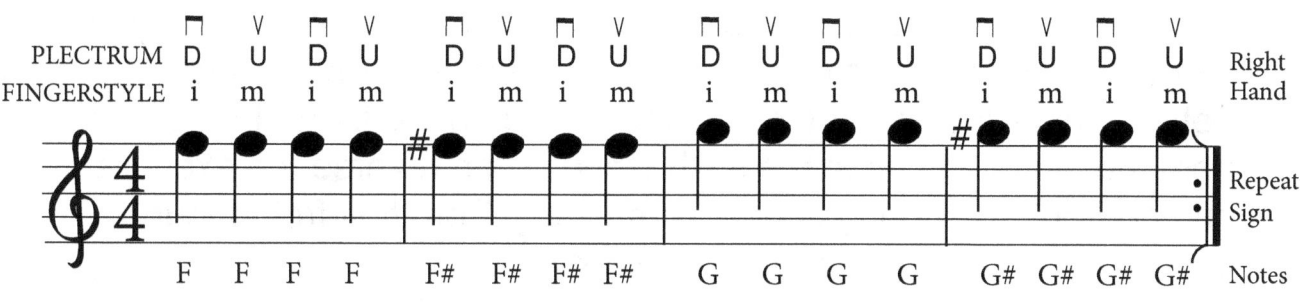

Fig.26

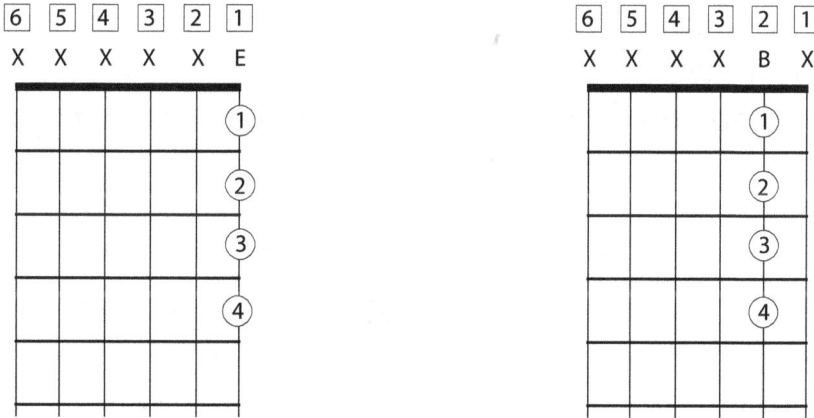

Fig.26A   *Fig.27A*

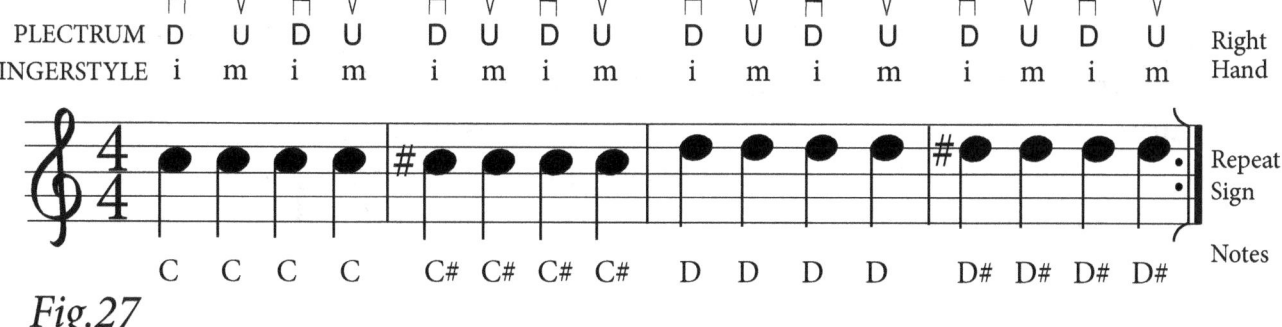

Fig.27

29

Exercise 5:
Play the notes in exercise 2, starting on the first string and going from the first fret to the fourth fret; then jumping to the third string and playing from the first fret to the fourth; then jumping to the second string and playing from the first fret to the fourth; and then jumping to the fourth string playing from the first fret to the fourth.

Exercise 6:
In Fig.28 play the notes in exercise 2, this time only once instead of four times. Play one note on the first fret, one note on the second fret, one note on the third fret and one note on the fourth fret, going from the first string up to the sixth string. Then reverse the exercise and go from sixth string down to first string, from first fret to fourth fret on each string, playing once per fret.

Exercise 7:
In Fig.29 play the notes one per fret (as in exercise 6), this time alternating the frets, going from the first fret to the third fret then to the second fret and to the fourth fret, and from the first string up to the sixth. Then reverse the exercise and go from the sixth string back down to the first string alternating the frets on each string.

Exercise 8:
Play the notes one per fret (as in exercise 6), also alternating the frets, this time going from the first fret to the fourth fret to the second fret and then to the third fret. Again go from the first string up to the sixth and then reverse the exercise and go back down to the first string.

These exercises not only gets you to practice your right and left hand techniques, but also allows you to start looking at the notes on the staff and adds an informal introduction into sight reading. Before going to the next exercise make sure that you are playing the exercise smoothly and in time with the metronome, and once that is achieved you could increase the speed of the metronome and practice to faster speeds.

Fig.28

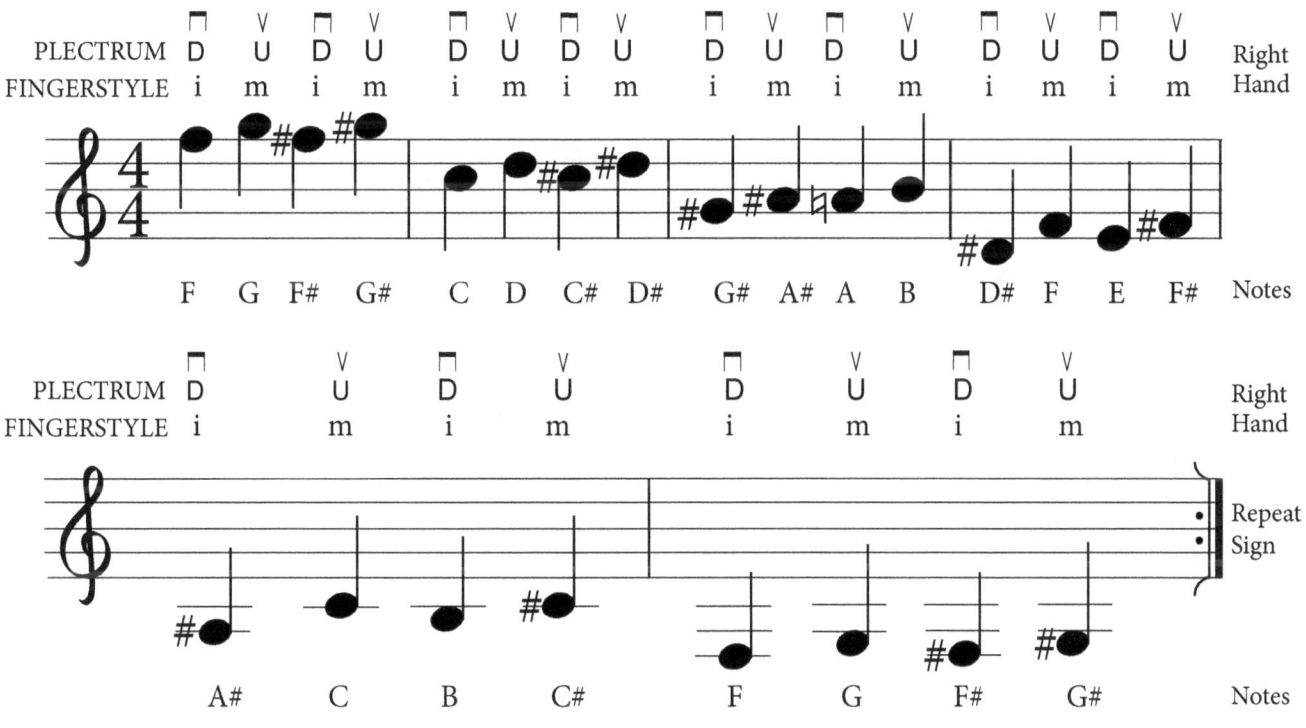

Fig.29

9 - Sight Reading 101

You have learnt the musical notes and have touched on the notes on the first four frets of the fretboard. You have also learnt left and right hand techniques. Now we shall combine them all in this section. In the following exercises are short melodies of songs which you will sight read and play. Most of the melodies you may be familiar with, so you may already have an idea of the melodies. You can go back to any section to review if you run into a mental block. As always, tune your guitar and put the metronome on 40 before you begin, take your time and concentrate, you cannot rush these. We all started the same way, not knowing how to play. Some notes such as the 'A' above the staff shall be played on the fifth fret.

Baa Baa Black Sheep

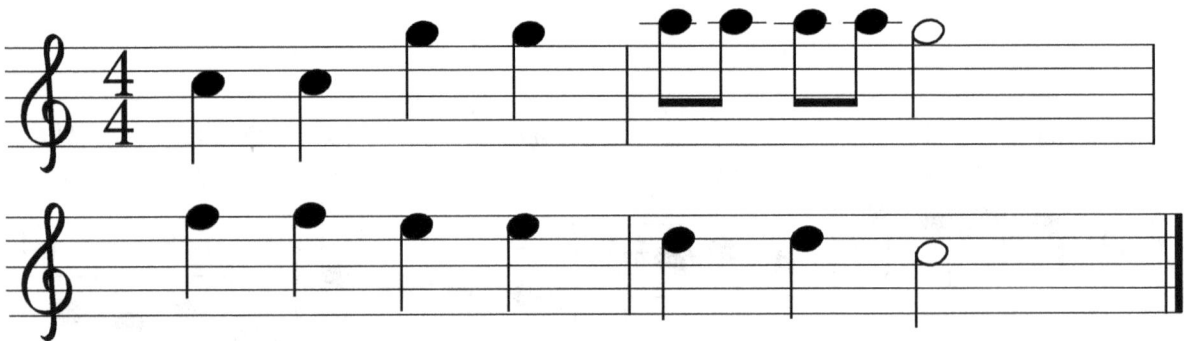

Fig.30

Jingle Bells

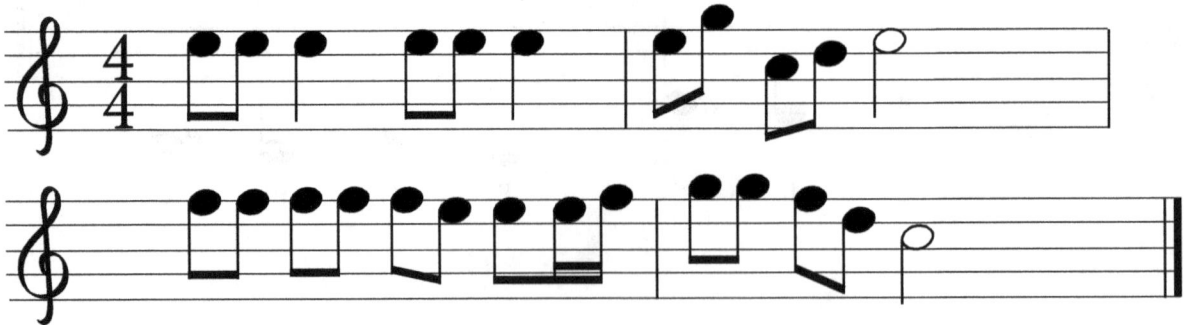

Fig.31

Mary Had A Little Lamb

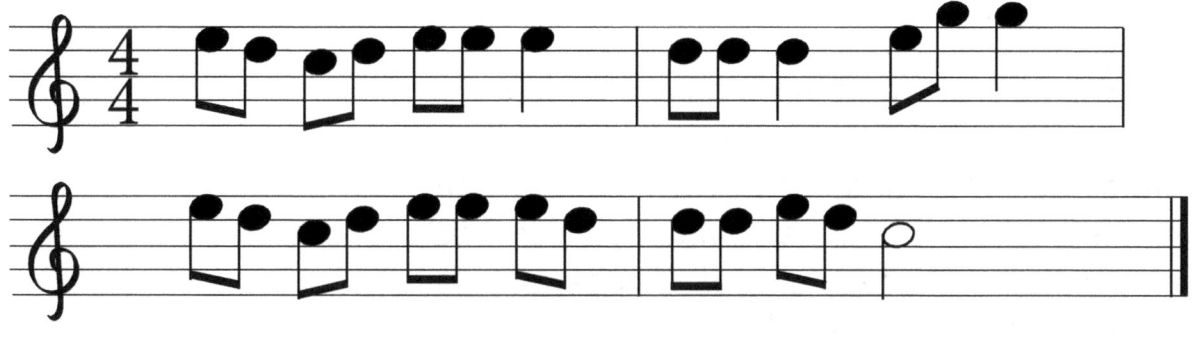

Fig.32

This Old Man

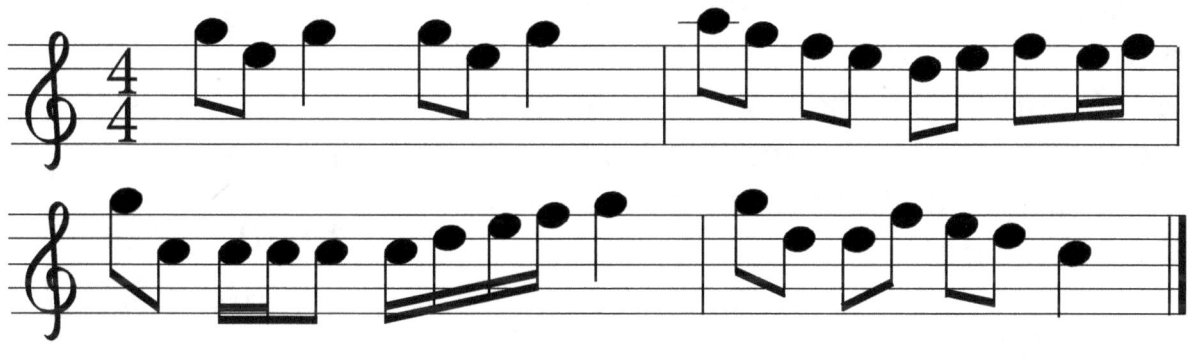

Fig.32

Then There's Ten

John Sebastian Gaskin
© 2013 BMI

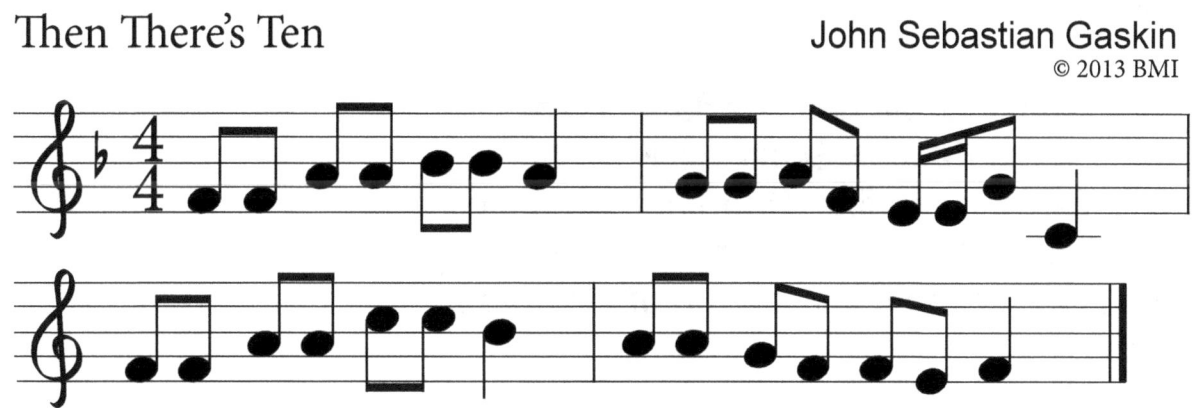

Fig.34

10 - Chords 101

We will be looking at three note chords in this book, called **Triads**. We will look at the **Major** (M - Maj) and **Minor** (m - min) Chords in this section. We are showing open chords, also called bottleneck chords. These chords are fingered at the top of the neck at the nut and employ the use of 'open' strings.

The **Chords** are built on the Root, Third and Fifth notes of the scale it represents (Fig.14 and Fig.15). The C-Major Scale has no sharp or flats. In the Music Theory section we see that the notes in the C-Major Scale are **C**-D-**E**-F-**G**-A-B-C. C is the first (Root) note, E is the third note and G is the fifth note of the scale. So the C-Major chord is made up of the notes C-E-G.

The G-Major Scale has one sharp (#). The notes in the G-Major Scale are **G**-A-**B**-C-**D**-E-F#-G. G is the first (Root) note, B is the third note and D is the fifth note of the scale. The G-Major chord is made up of the notes G-B-D.

The F-Major Scale has one flat ($\flat$). The notes in the F-Major Scale are **F**-G-**A**-B$\flat$-**C**-D-E-F. F is the first (Root) note, A is the third note and C is the fifth note of the scale. The F-Major chord is made up of the notes F-A-C.

In a Major Chord the interval between the first (root) note and the second note is a

"Chords are harmonic structures. They are used to accompany melodies or vocals. Chords can be two notes and up to six on the guitar."

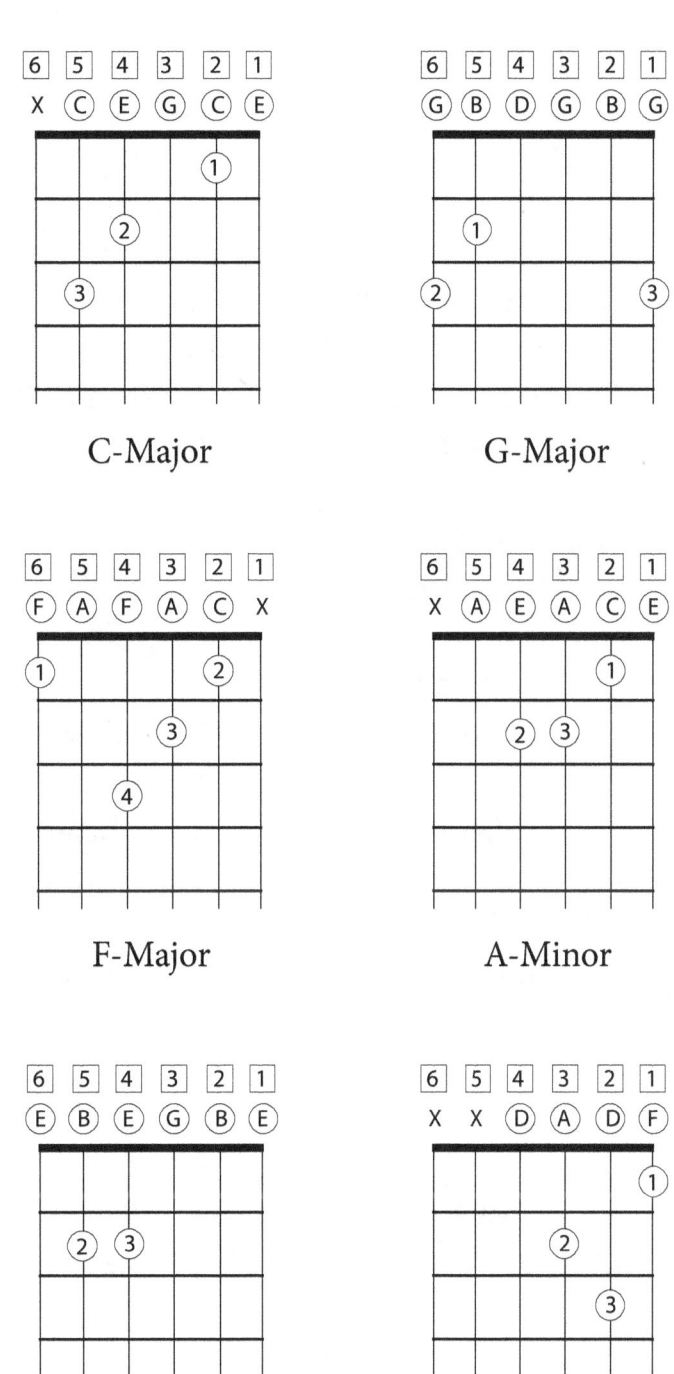

"The 'X' above the nut indicates that that string should not be played (muted). The notes above the nut are the notes in the chord being played."

'major third'. The interval between the first (root) note and the third note is a 'perfect fifth', shown in the Music Theory 101 section. C-Major can also be written CM or CMaj.

To create a Minor chord from a Major chord, lower the third note of the scale a half step. On the guitar that is moving back one fret, essentially flattening the note. C-Minor (Cm or Cmin) notes are C-E♭-G. In a Minor Chord the interval between the first (root) note and the second note is a **Minor Third**. The interval between the first (root) note and the third note remains a **Perfect Fifth**.

In the Music Theory 101 section we mentioned that there are no sharp or flats between the notes B-C and E-F. Again, they do occur. If one is to call out the notes in a D-Minor chord they will be D-F-A. If one asks for the notes of a D-flat Minor chord the notes will be D♭-F♭-A♭. Here we have an F♭ because we have to keep the designation of 'F' in the chord. If we called the note 'E' it would be referring to a chord other than D♭ Minor.

In all the chords shown we have kept the lowest (bass) note as the root note of the chord. These chords are useful when accompanying a vocalist or single melody.

"There are different inversions of each chord that allows the player to access the same chord at different parts of the fretboard."

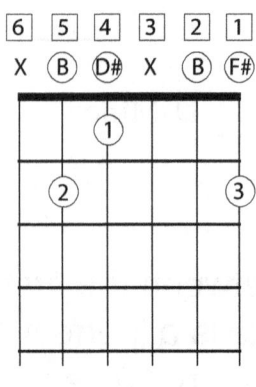

B-Major

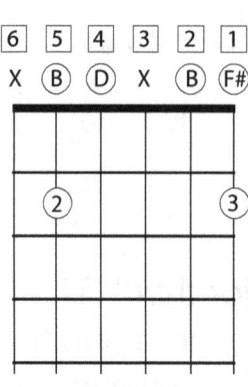

B-Minor

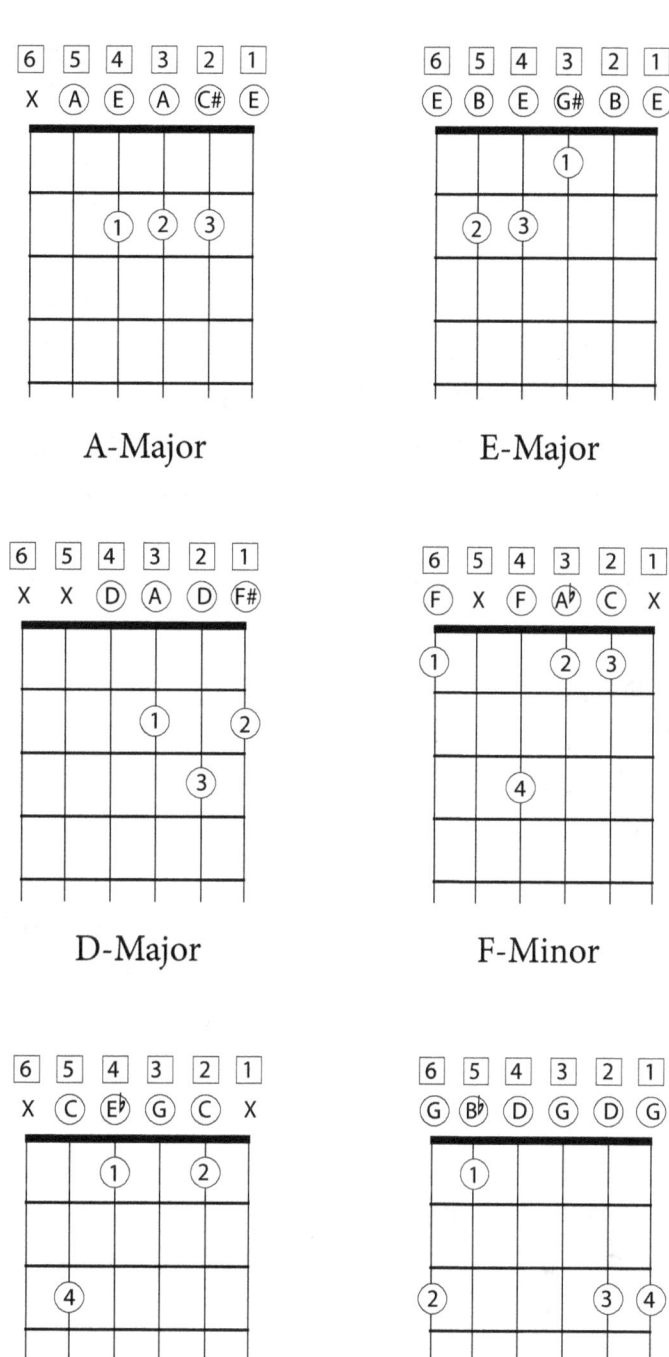

"These Chords are 'triads', chords with three diatonic tones from the scale degree they are representing, and are classified by their root note."

When practicing the chords play each string separately, one after the other (arpeggio). This will allow you, the student, to hear which strings are not being pressed properly and to work on improving that note.

11 - Chord Exercises 101

In this section we will be looking at chords and a few progressions of different rhythmic patterns to get you into the other aspect of the guitar, rhythm. Guitarists play a combination of rhythm guitar and lead guitar. Lead guitar exercises have been presented in the Fretboard Exercises 101 section. As mentioned previously, rhythm is a very fundamental and important aspect in music. Different cultures have their own rhythmic expression in their national music, which differentiates one from the other. So there is a lot to learn if the student wishes to pursue the guitar as a profession.

One way of learning music is by listening. The student should listen to other guitarists to hear how they play. The student should also listen to drummers and keyboardists to hear how they play, their rhythmic expressions and feel.

Two ways of playing chords are strumming and arpeggio. It depends on the style of music and feel of the composition that may determine which is used. In the Chords 101 section we showed the C-Major chord. We will start by using this chord as we show the different rhythms and patterns, and we will start with strumming. Fingerstyle players should use the thumb on their right hand for strumming while others will use the pick. All rhythmic values will be similar to that of musical notes, as shown by their stems.

Exercise 1:
In Fig.35 this exercise all strokes will be played with the downstroke. Play the C-Major chord four times in each measure on the beat with the metronome and repeat until the sound is clear and the rhythm is smooth. Then practice the other chords you have just learnt.

Exercise 2:
In Fig.36 quarter rests have replaced some of the strokes in exercise 1. The pattern may look difficult but it is the same stroke pattern repeated, play two then rest for one, play two then rest for one.

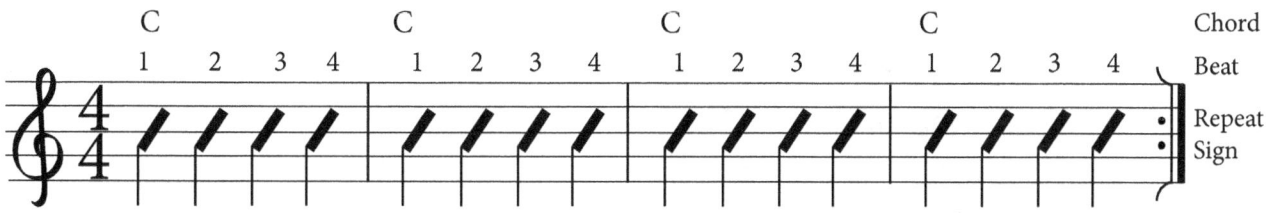

Fig.35

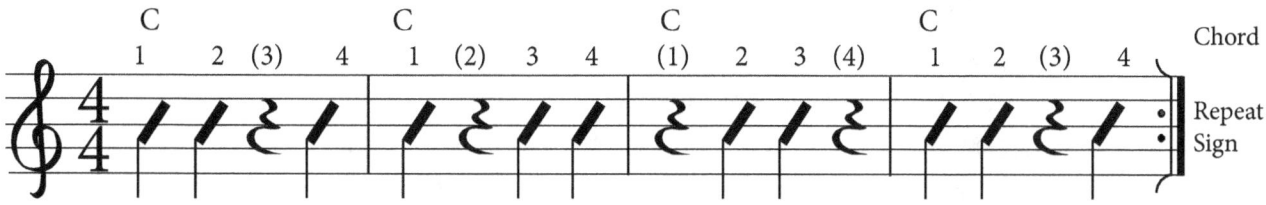

Fig.36

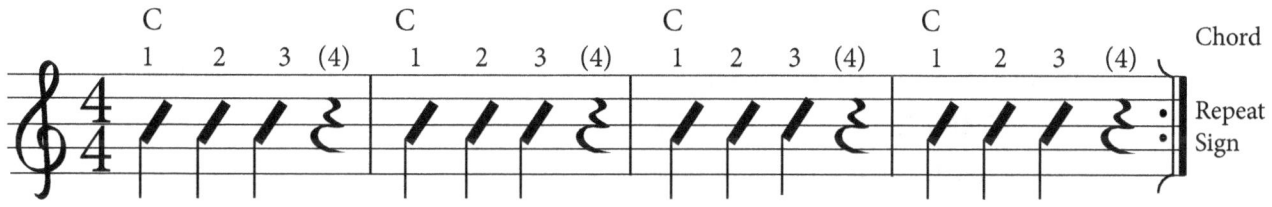

Fig.37

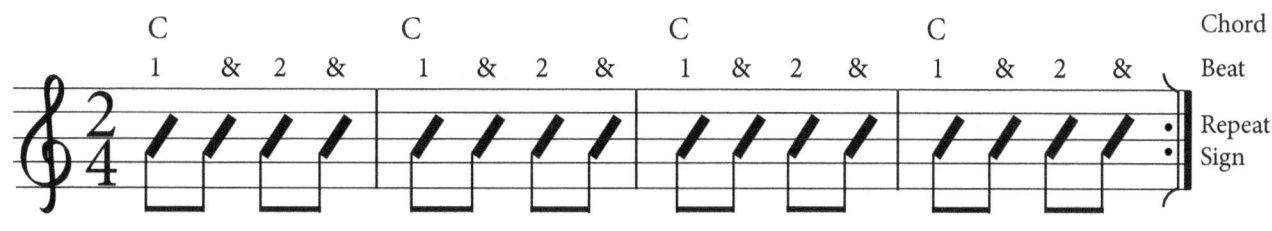

Fig.38

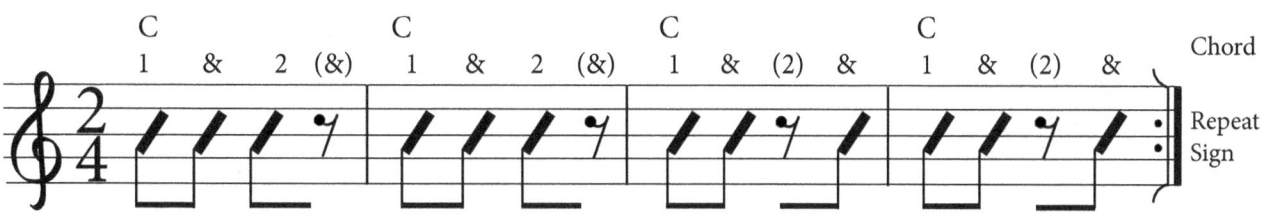

Fig.39

Exercise 3:
In Fig.37, like in exercise 2, quarter rests have replaced some of the strokes. Here the pattern looks easier as the rest falls in the same place in each measure and the same stroke pattern is repeated, play three then rest for one, play three then rest for one.

Exercise 4:
In Fig.38 the time signature has changed, the beat is still the quarter note like the previous exercises. Now we have introduced the eight note rhythm, which breaks the beat into two. In this exercise the rhythm is now down on the beat and up on the 'and', no longer all downbeats. So for each measure the student plays a downstroke, followed by and upstroke, followed by another downstroke and then another upstroke.

Exercise 5:
In Fig.39 we added the "eight" rest to break up the rhythm. The rhythmic pattern here is down-up-down-rest, down-up-down-rest, down-up-rest-up, down-up-rest-up. Go slowly until you feel the rhythm, then you can speed up the metronome to get a different feel.

Exercise 6:
In Fig.40 we have added other chords from the previous Chord 101 section. The chords will go through a series of progressions, which the student will play and concentrate on changing from one chord to another as smoothly as possible.

Exercise 7:
Fig.41 is similar to exercise 6 with a different chord progression to continue to help the student practice chords and changing from one chord to another.

Exercise 8:
In Fig.42 we show a few chords creating a chord progression in the way a student may find on some song sheets. This exercise is to encourage the students to play whatever rhythm they choose. Keep the beat and move smoothly between chords.

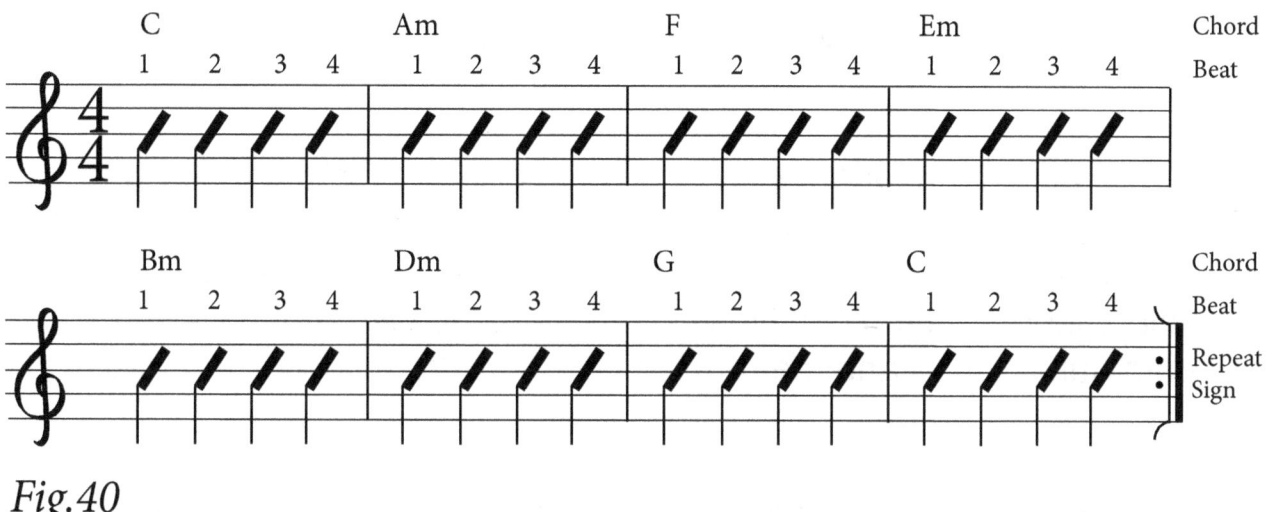

Fig.40

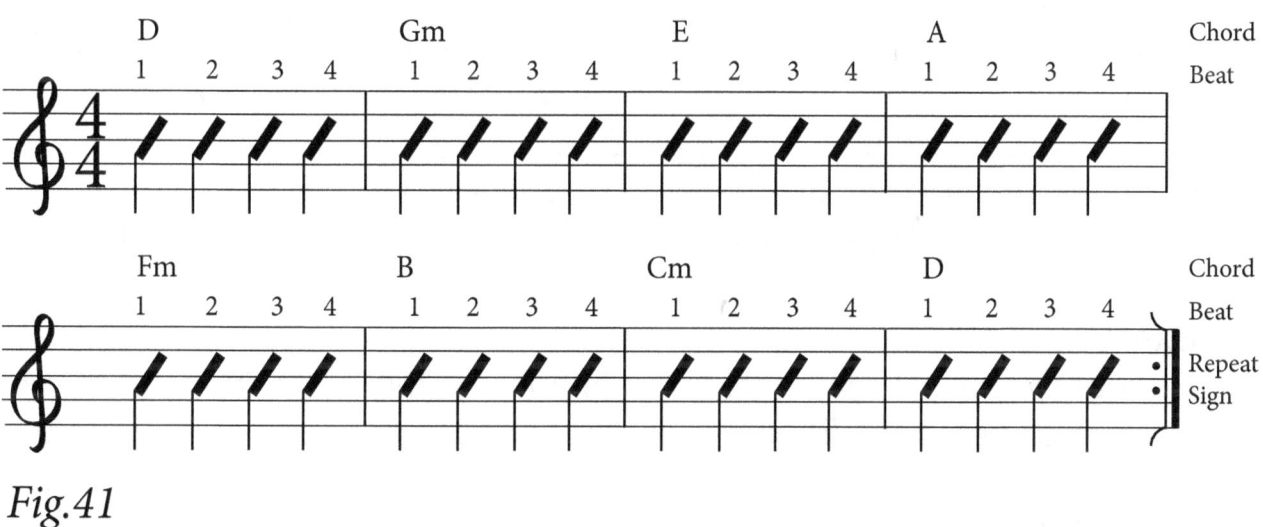

Fig.41

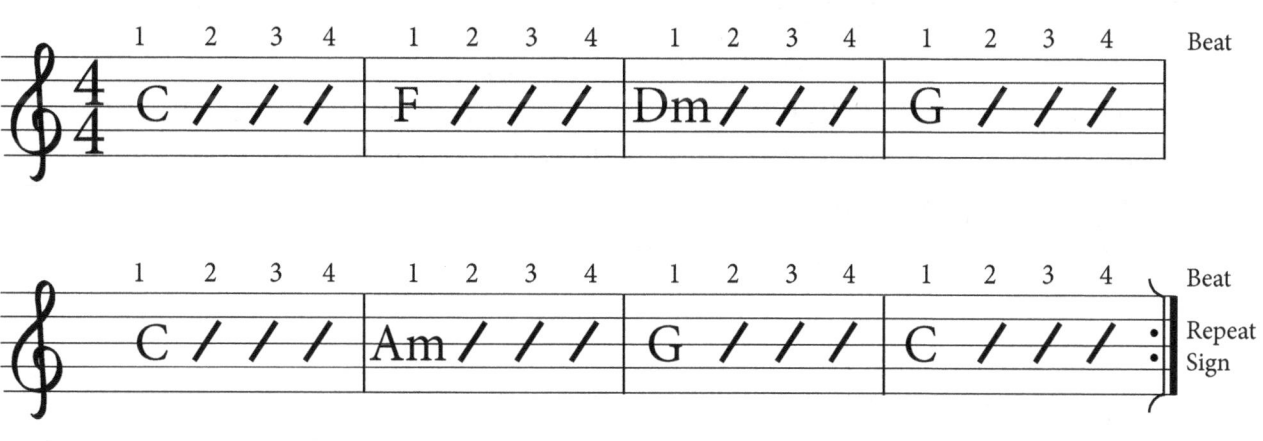

Fig.42

12 - Fretboard Exercises 102

At this point the student should be comfortable with the guitar and playing. When playing the exercises in the Fretboard Exercises 101 section your left hand fingers may have stayed bunched together to help support each other. Here you will practice finger independence. With guitar tuned and metronome on - play the following exercises.

Exercise 1:
Using Fig.43 place your first finger at the first fret on the first string and play that note (F). Put your second finger at the second fret, leaving your first finger in place and play that note (F#). Put your third finger at the third fret, leaving the first two in place and play that note (G). Put your fourth finger at the fourth fret, leaving the other three in place and play that note (G#). Repeat this on the second, third, fourth, fifth and sixth strings. Reverse the exercise and play from the sixth string down to the first string and first fret to fourth.

Exercise 2:
Repeat exercise 1, going from the fifth fret to the eight and then try the twelfth fret to the fifteenth. The fret spaces get smaller as you go down the fretboard. This will give your finger a chance to feel out the guitar and also be more comfortable with the exercise.

Exercise 3:
Using Fig.43, the student will play one note per fret, going from fourth fret to first starting on the first string then go up to the sixth string and then back down to the first string. This time the student using the plectrum will start with a downstroke followed by a upstroke. Those playing fingerstyle will play start with the middle (m) finger move backwards (m-a-m-i).

Exercise 4:
Using Fig.44, the student will play one note per fret with alternate fingering of the left hand, going from first string up to sixth, then back down to the first string. This time the students using

Fig.43

Fig.44

the plectrum shall use the picking technique of up-down-down-up. Those playing fingerstyle will use the four fingers of their right hand, the index (i), middle (m), ring (a) and little finger (c) for this exercise. Go slowly, take your time, practice-practice-practice, you will get it.

Now, we will start practicing **Scales** using the first six frets of the guitar. These exercises will employ, alternating down-up strokes, with the plectrum and alternating between index and middle fingers for fingerstyle players. These exercises will go from the sixth string down to the first string and back up to the sixth string.

Exercise 5:
Using Fig.45 and Fig.45A this exercise is to practice the G-Major Scale, starting on the third fret on the sixth string, with the root note of the scale, G. This scale has one sharp, F#. This G note is located just below middle C on the guitar and musical staff. This scale position is referred to as the - first position, sixth string, G-Major.

Exercise 6:
Using Fig.46 and Fig.46A this exercise is the C-Major Scale, starting on the third fret on the fifth string, with the root note of the scale, C. This scale has no sharps or flats, all notes are natural. This note is middle C. This scale position is referred to as the - first position, fifth string, C-Major. This scale does not go two full octaves as we are just playing on the first six frets.

Exercise 7:
Using Fig.47 and Fig.47A this exercise is the A-Minor Scale, starting on the fifth fret of the sixth string. If one compares this scale to the C-Major scale in Fig.46 and Fig.46A, you will notice that it has the same notes. The difference is that this scale starts on the scale root note of 'A'. A-minor is the relative minor of C-Major, which means literally that they are related. 'A' is the sixth scale degree (note) of the C-Major scale and is referred to as the Aeolian Scale or Relative Minor Scale. Other minor scales are the Minor Pentatonic (blues), Harmonic and Melodic. We will not be looking at them in this book.

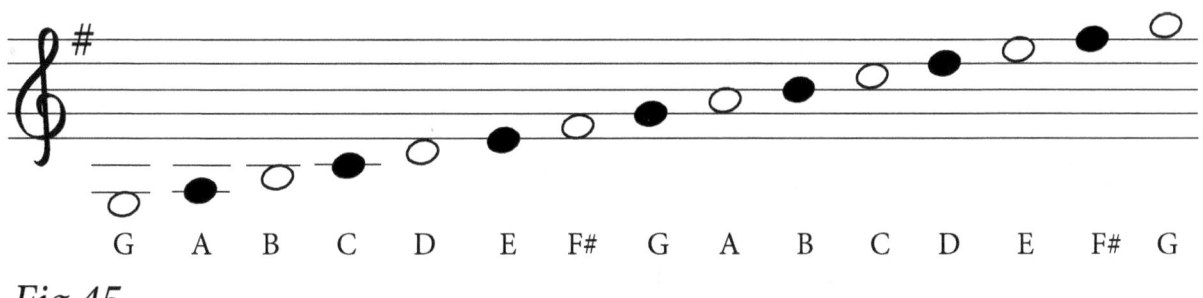

Fig.45

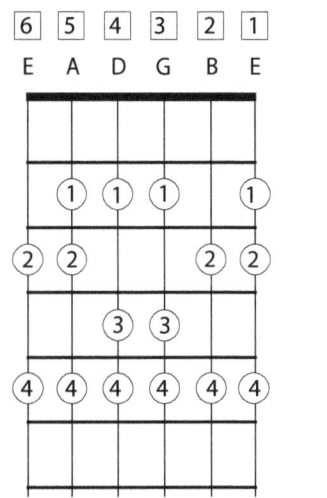

Fig.45A

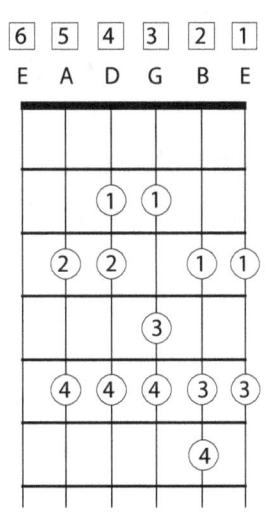

Fig.46A

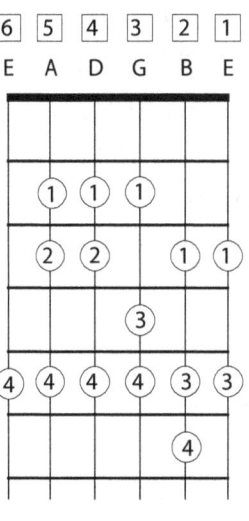

Fig.47A

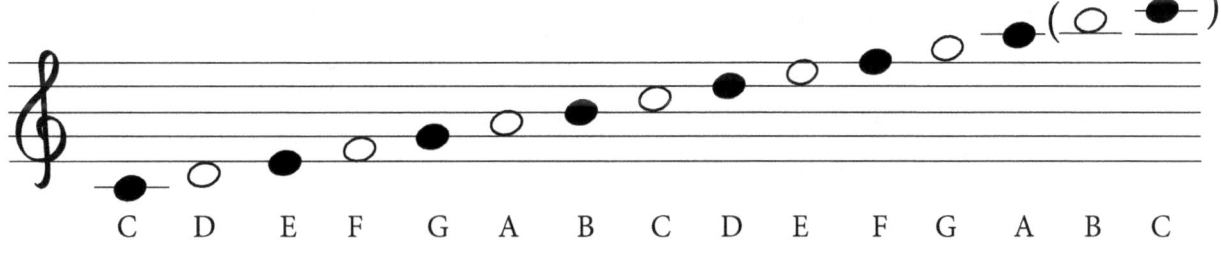

Fig.46

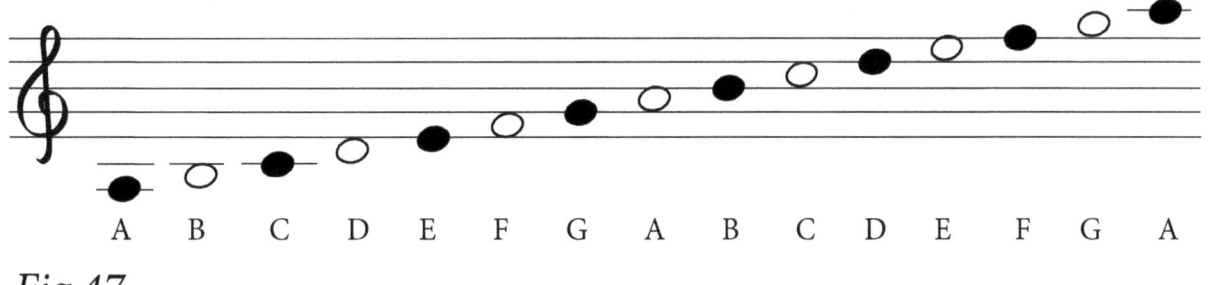

Fig.47

13 - Chords 102

In the Music Theory 101 section we learnt the intervals of a major scale. **Chords** that are built from the root, fourth or fifth notes (scale degrees) of a major scale will always produce Major chords. Chords built from the second, third or sixth notes of the major scale produce Minor chords. Chords built from the seventh note of a major scale produces a **Diminished** chord. The scale degree note the chord is built from becomes the root of that chord.

The seventh of a B♭ scale is A (Fig.15, Music Theory 101 section). A chord built on 'A' will give the notes A-C-E♭, an A-Diminished chord. In a Diminished Chord the interval between the first (root) note and the second note is a 'minor third'. The interval between the first (root) note and the third note is a 'tritone', flatted fifth. The Diminish Chord is seen as a minor chord with the fifth flattened. There are two intervals of minor thirds (three semi-tones) between the notes.

Diminished chords normally resolve, or move, to the one (root) chord, which is aided by the leading tone of the scale moving to be resolved. In the C-Major scale the B (seventh note) resolves to the C (root). In this case the seventh note resolves up to the octave. The Diminished Chord seems to function like a Dominant Chord (chords built on the fifth scale degree). They both want to go to another chord to resolve.

"Some chords will be easier to play than others at the beginning, until you have practiced and have made some progress with your fingering."

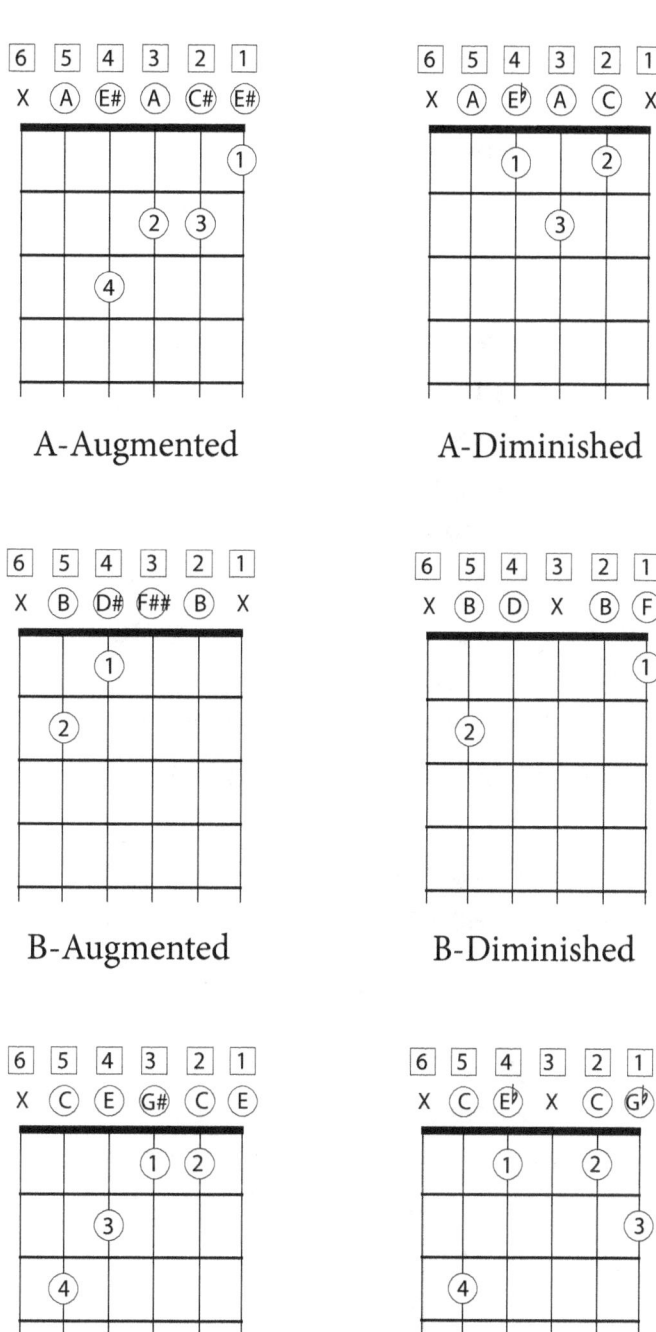

"Diminished Chords are considered a type of Minor Chord, and Augmented Chords are considered a type of Major Chord."

Another resolution is the fourth scale tone, which resolves down to the third scale tone. Chords easily resolves to another if there is at least one common tone in each. Many times a resolution is not as expected.

The **Diminished** and **Augmented** chords have unique sounds. They create tension and they sound unresolved. They need to go to another chord to finish 'the idea'. They are used mainly as passing chords.

The Augmented Chord is not part of the scale degree theory. An Augmented Chord built from the note F of the B♭ scale will give the notes F-A-C#. In an Augmented Chord the interval between the first (root) note and the second note is a 'major third'. The interval between the first (root) note and the third note is a 'augmented fifth', sharpened fifth. The C# note is not in the key of B♭. The Augmented chord is seen as a Major Chord with the fifth sharpened, or moved up a semi-tone. There are two intervals of major thirds, four semi-tones (two whole tones) between the notes.

Modern day music have accepted these chords and have used them in different ways other than a resolution to other chords.

"Leading Tones are notes of the seventh scale degree that are a half-step away from the tonic note it resolves towards in the next chord."

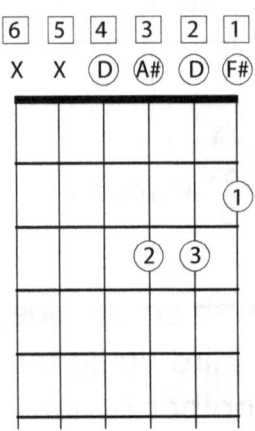
D-Augmented

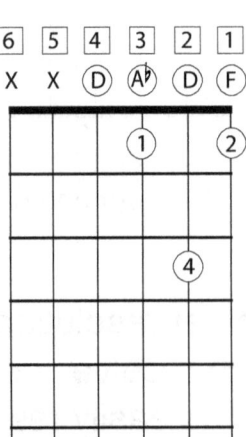
D-Diminished

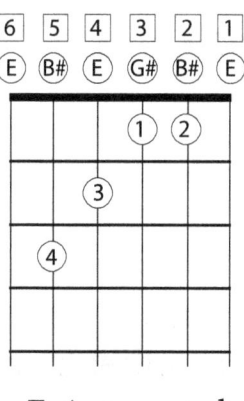
E-Augmented

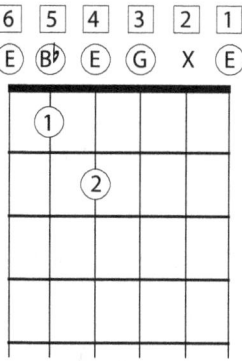
E-Diminished

"*In the early years of music the Diminished Chord was considered 'Devil Music'. It created a dissonant sound, a tritone interval, that was not accepted.*"

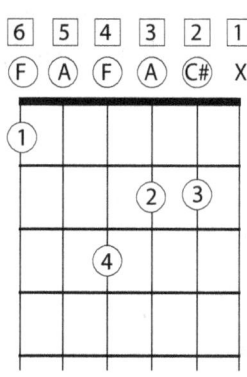
F-Augmented

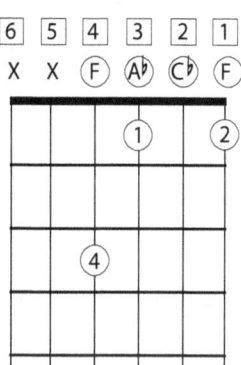
F-Diminished

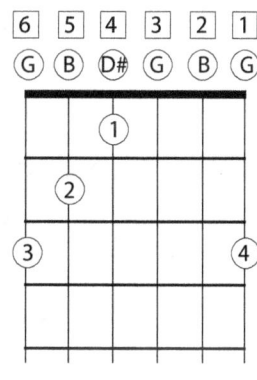
G-Augmented

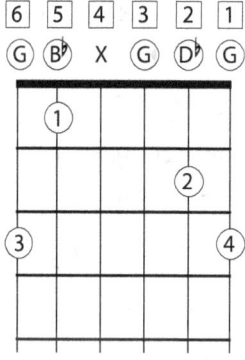
G-Diminished

When practicing these chords make sure that the changes, from one chord to the another, is smooth and even. You have learnt the four chord qualities of the triad; Major, Minor, Augmented and Diminished.

14 - Chord Exercises 102

In the Chord Exercises 101 section we looked at the art of strumming the guitar to play chords with some rhythmic patterns. In this section we will be looking at arpeggios (broken chords). Fingerstyle students will now use the thumb of their right hand to pluck the lower strings and the other fingers will play the higher strings. In these exercises the student will use one right hand finger per string. Students using the pick will continue using the pick to play the notes in the chord, moving from string to string. As usual, tune up, put on the metronome and take your time.

Exercise 1:
In Fig.48 using the C-Major chord again, fingerstyle students will use the right hand to play the fifth string note, C, with the thumb (P). The index finger (i) will play the third string, G, and middle finger (m) will play the second string, C. The ring finger (a) will play the first string, E. Each note will be played on the beat. The left hand position stay the same as learnt previously in the Chords 101 section. Plectrum players will play the fifth, third, second and first strings using all downstrokes. The fourth string is not to be played. It is to be muted.

Exercise 2:
In Fig.49 we will use the A-Minor chord. Fingerstyle students will use the same pattern as in exercise-1 as we stay on the fifth, third, second and first strings. Some of the notes have been changed. The left hand position is the same as learnt previously in the Chords 101 section. Plectrum players will use the same pattern as in exercise-1, all downstrokes. Again the fourth string is not to be played.

Exercise 3:
In Fig.50 we will be using the G-Major chord, playing the sixth, fourth, third and second strings. We have added a more arpeggiated pattern and there has been a slight change to the music score. The bass note has a separate staff part and is independent of the upper notes and held. The stems for the upper notes are shown all in one

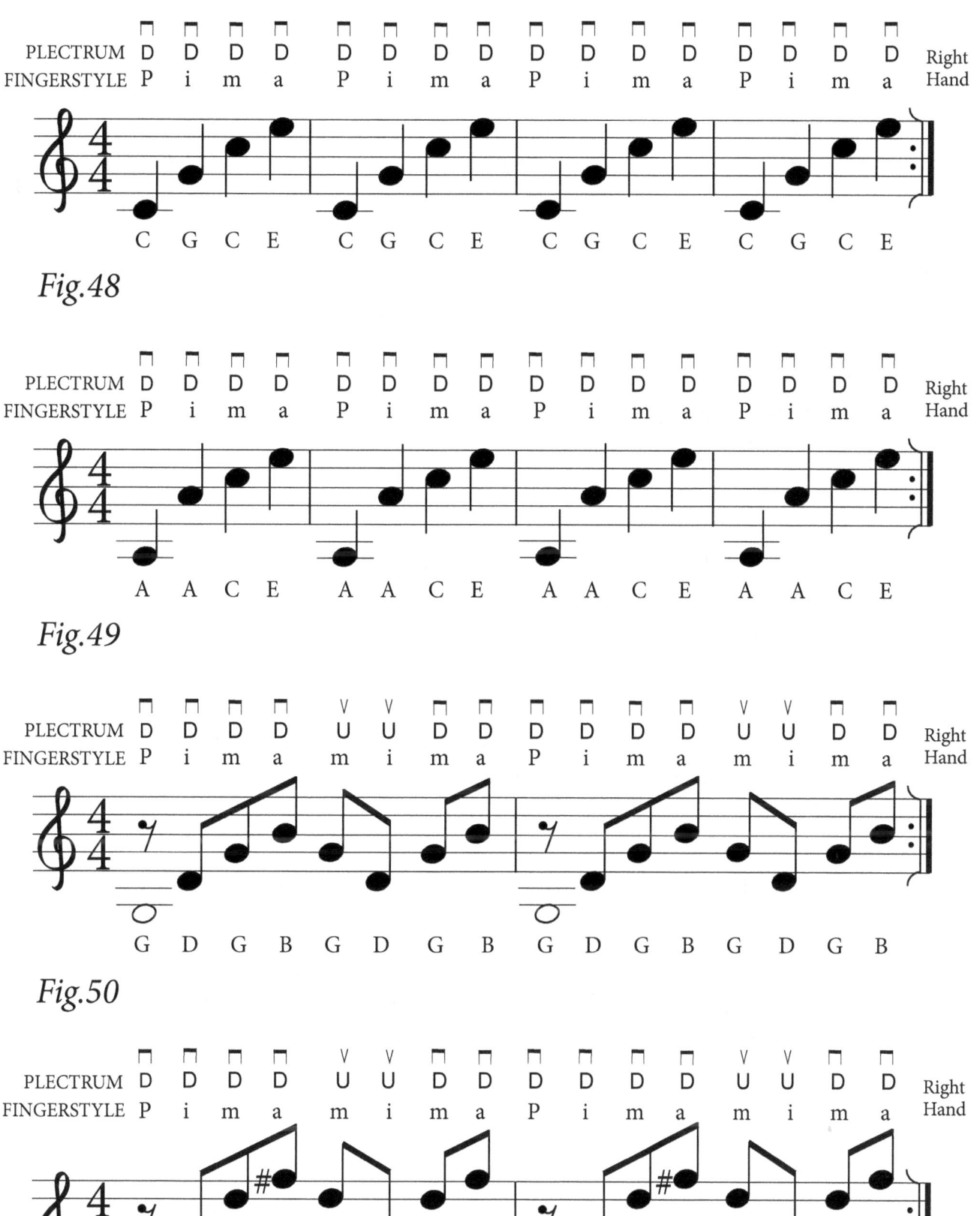

Fig.48

Fig.49

Fig.50

Fig.51

direction unlike previous musical scores. The right hand fingering pattern has been extended. The picking (plectrum) technique is now downstrokes from fourth string to second, upstrokes on the third and fourth strings and downstokes back to second string. Eight notes have been introduced and some notes do not occur on the beat.

Exercise 4:
In Fig.51 we will be using the D Major chord. We will be playing the fourth, third, second and first strings. The pattern is similar to exercise-3. Downstrokes on the third thru first strings, upstrokes on the second and third strings and again downstrokes to the first string.

Exercise 5:
In Fig.52 we will be playing progressions, the student gets to practice arpeggios going from chord to chord. Just as you did in the Chord Exercise 101 section with strumming. In this exercise we will not be showing the names of notes. By now the student should be able to recognize notes and values. The student needs to concentrate, take their time, so that they can also recognize the changes with the notes and as such the chords.

Exercise 6:
In Fig.53 this exercise is using 'eight' notes as in exercise 50 and 51. The right hand technique changes slightly. The fingerstyle students and those using the plectrum should review the fingering information above the staves for the right hand. The left hand techniques remain the same as they were learnt in the Chords 101 section. The bass pattern adds a second bass note, with either a finger from the left hand pressing the note or it is played as an open string.

You, the student, have learnt to play chords in both strumming and arpeggios styles. There is much more to be learnt. One exercise we have not touched on is playing melodies and chords together. The following Songs section shows melodies and chords, which you, the student, in your now ever growing prowess can tackle.

PLECTRUM D D D D D D D D D D D D D D D D
FINGERSTYLE P i m a P i m a P i m a P i m a
Right Hand
PLECTRUM D D D D D D D D D D D D D D D D
FINGERSTYLE P i m a P i m a P i m a P i m a
Right Hand

Fig.52

PLECTRUM D U D U D U D U D D D D U U D D
FINGERSTYLE P i m a P i a m P i m a P i a m
Right Hand
PLECTRUM D D D D U U D D D D D D U U D D
FINGERSTYLE P i m a P i a m P i m a P i a m
Right Hand

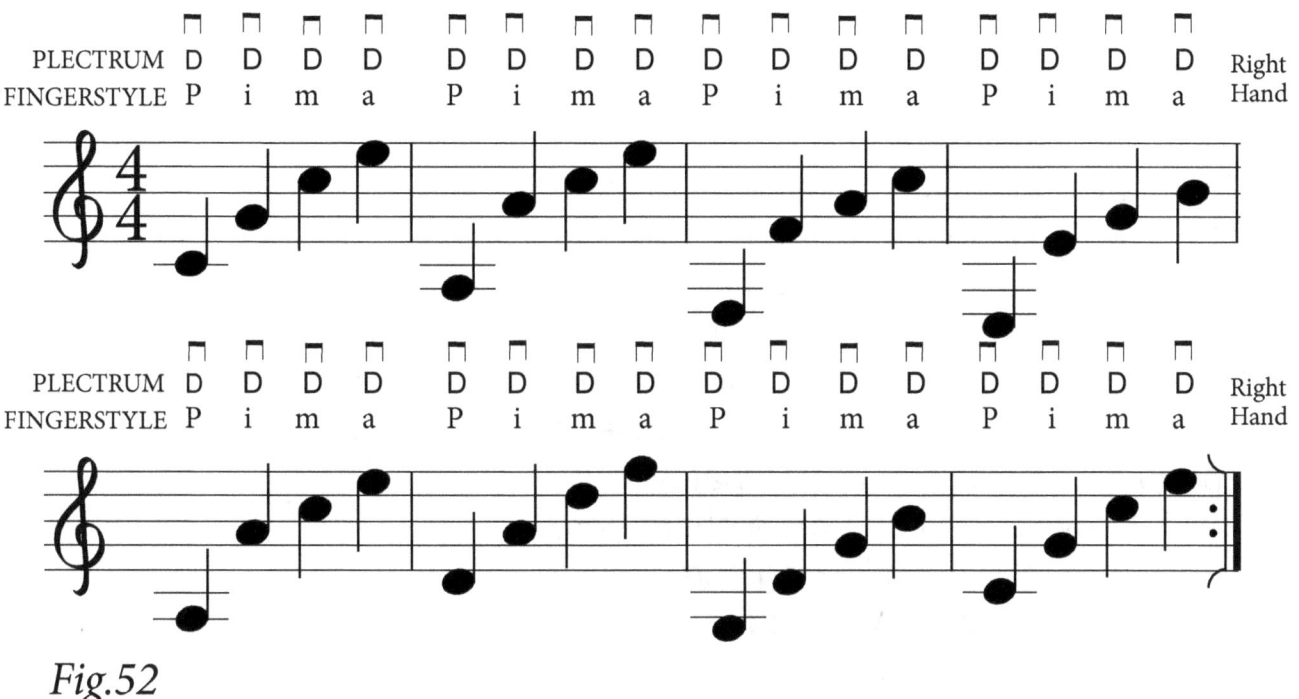

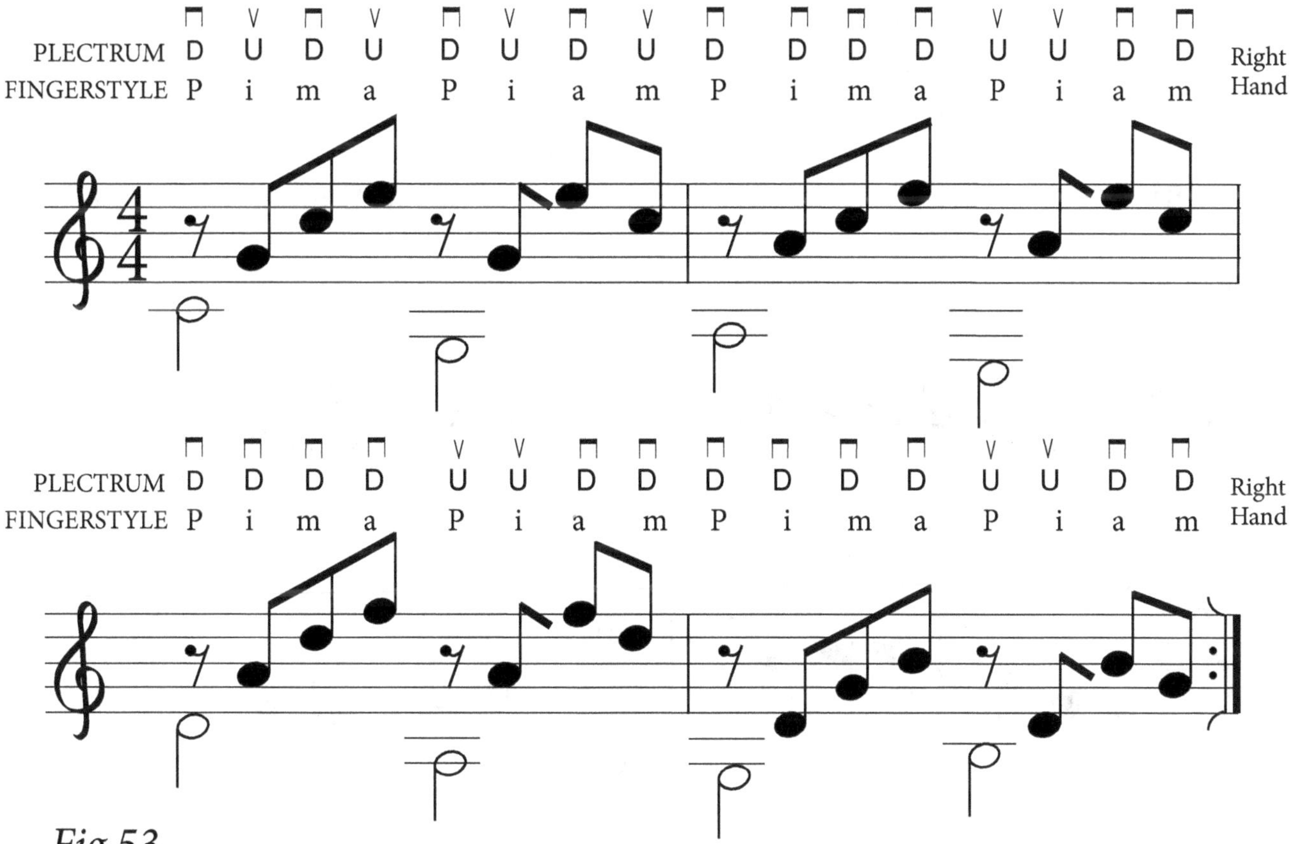

Fig.53

15 - Songs

Congratulations, you have come to the end of Guitar-1. Hopefully, you have made much progress in your learning to play the guitar, in music theory and sight reading. You can always go back over material in this book as you need to. You can now increase the speed of the metronome to whatever you want. I have added one extra chord here, B♭ Major. It is in the following composition. Here are some songs for you to practice with chords and melody. These types of music scores are called lead sheets. They do not tell the performer exactly how to play, just what to play. You can also obtain music sheets of songs you like to learn and play them. Enjoy.

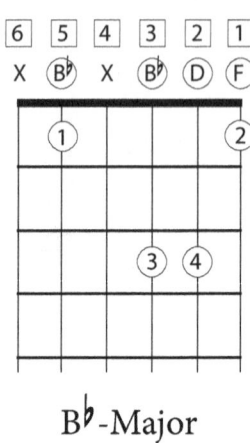

B♭-Major

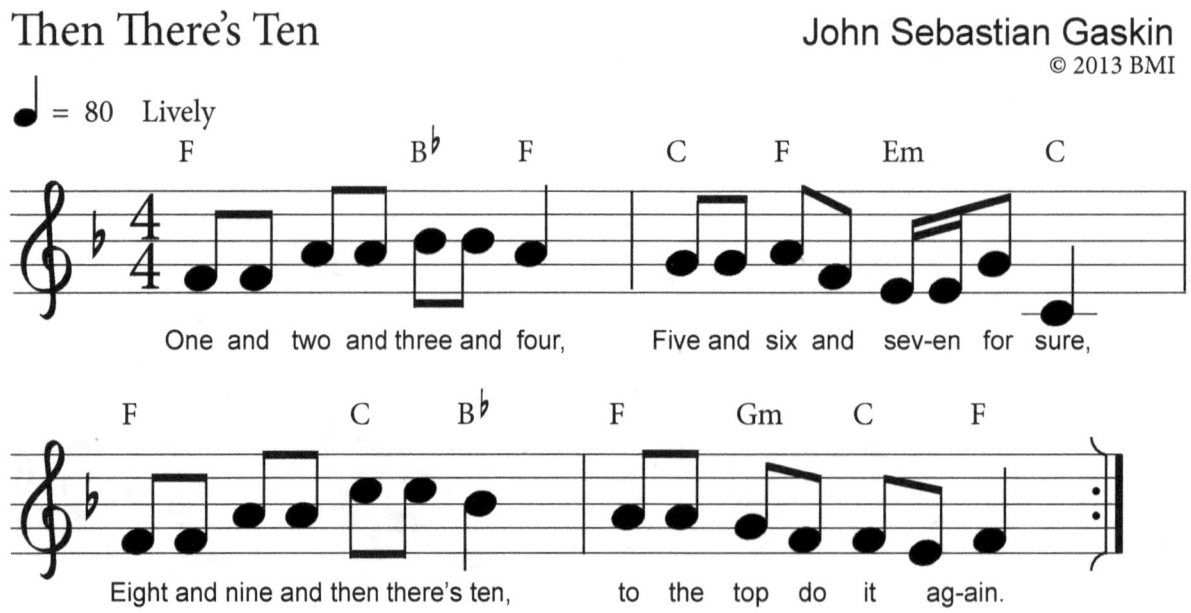

Fig.54

London Bridge

Claes Van Visscher
1616

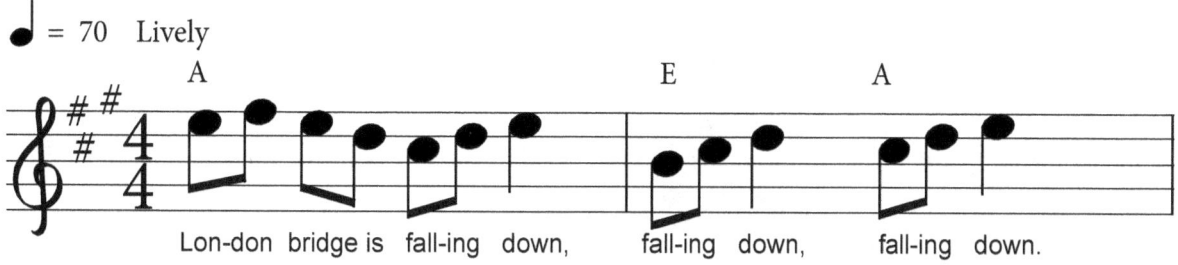

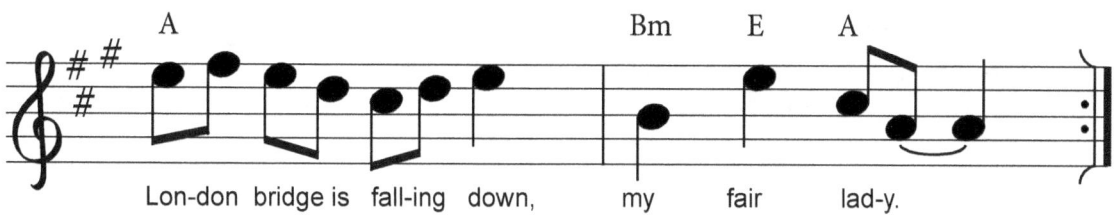

Fig.55

I Saw Three Ships

arr: John S. Gaskin
1833 - Originally in 6/8 timing

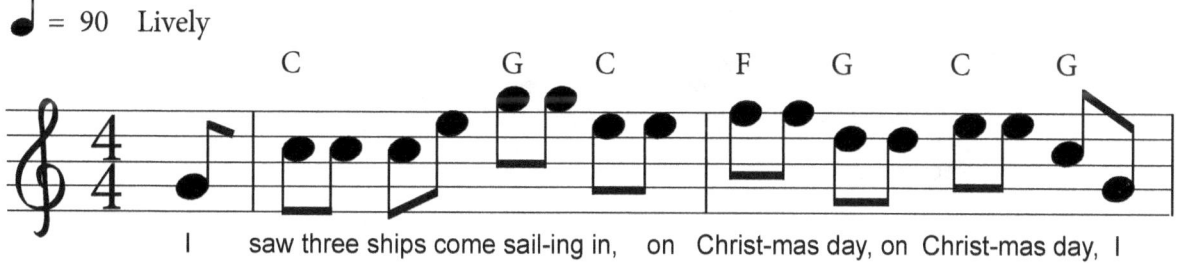

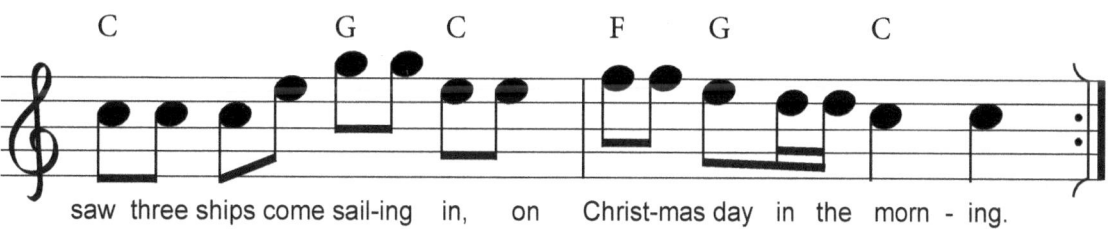

Fig.56

Old MacDonald Had A Farm

Traditional
1917

♩ = 70   Lively

Old Mac Don-ald had a farm,   eee-i eee-i O,   and

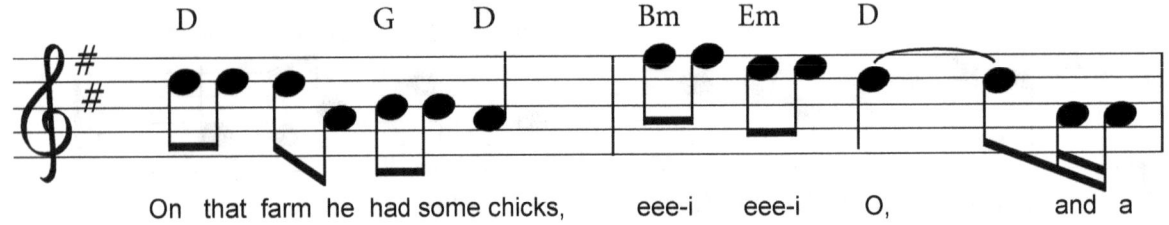

On that farm he had some chicks,   eee-i eee-i O,   and a

chick chick here and a chick chick there,   here a chick there a chick ev-ery where a chick chick.

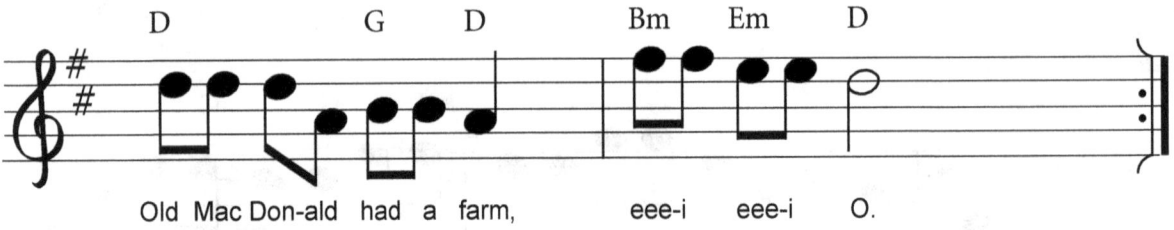

Old Mac Don-ald had a farm,   eee-i eee-i O.

Fig.57

Mary Had A Little Lamb

Lowell Mason
1830

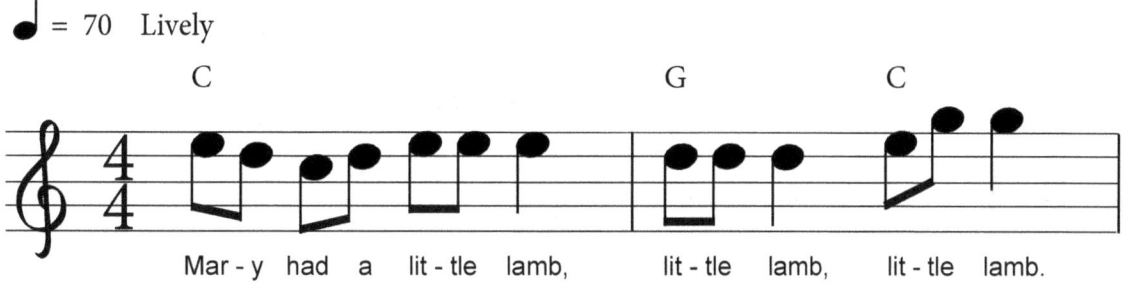

Fig.58

This Old Man

George Arthur Meyer
1906

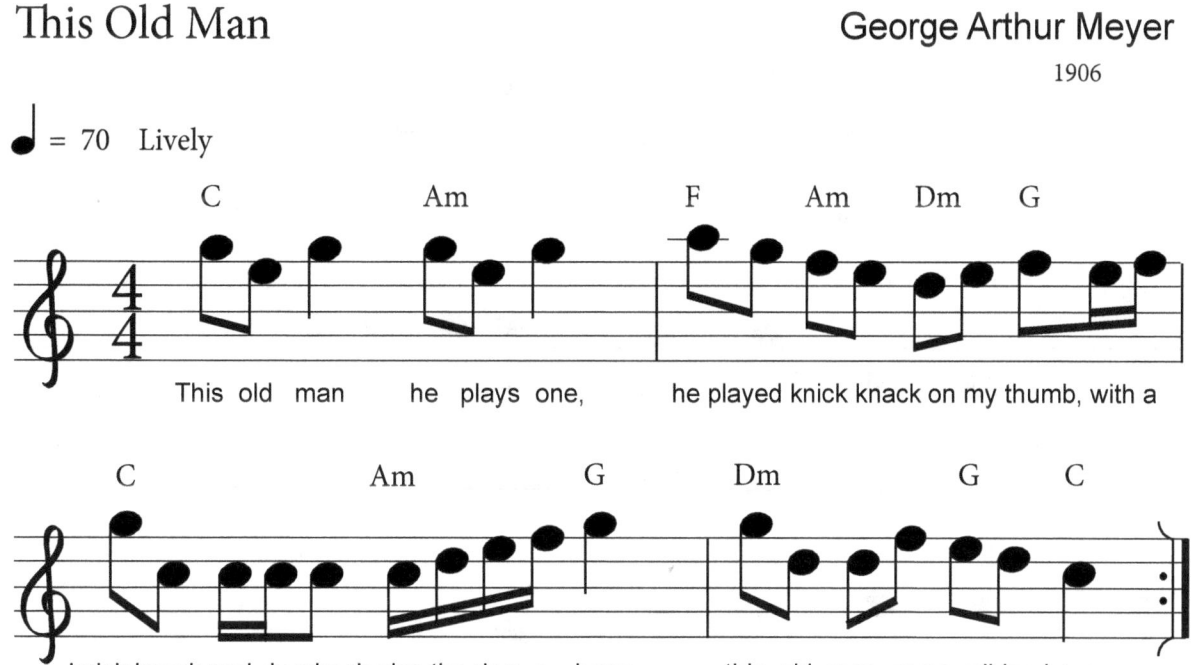

Fig.59

Baa Baa Black Sheep

Traditional
1744

Fig.60

We Three Kings

John H. Hopkins
1857

♩ = 70 Lively

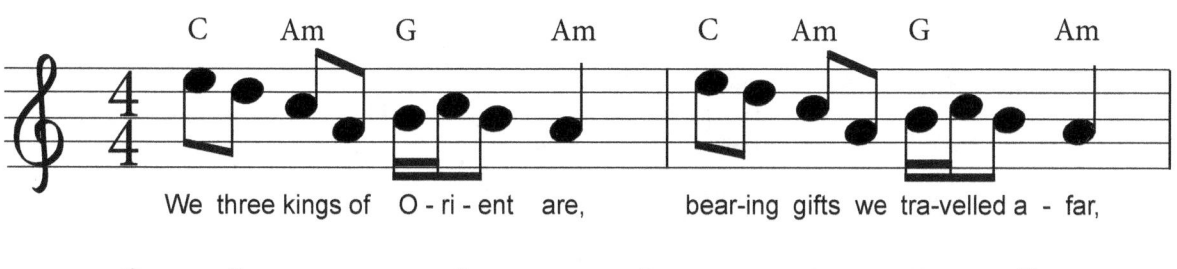
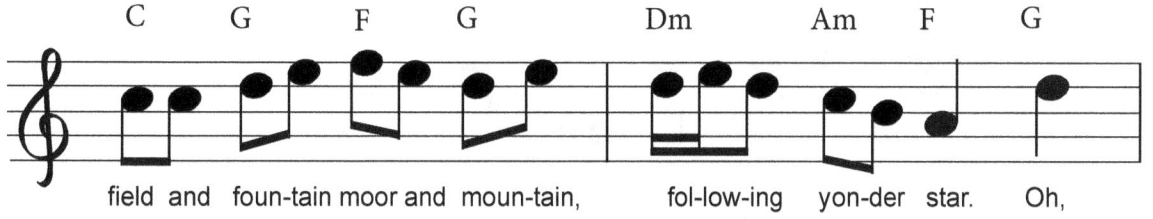
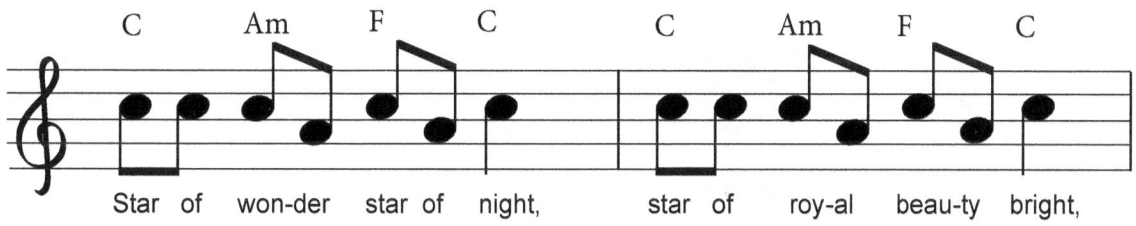
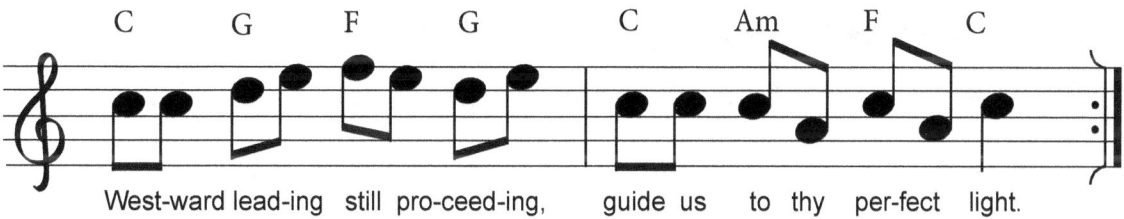

Fig.61

Jingle Bells

James Pierpont
1857

♩ = 70 Lively

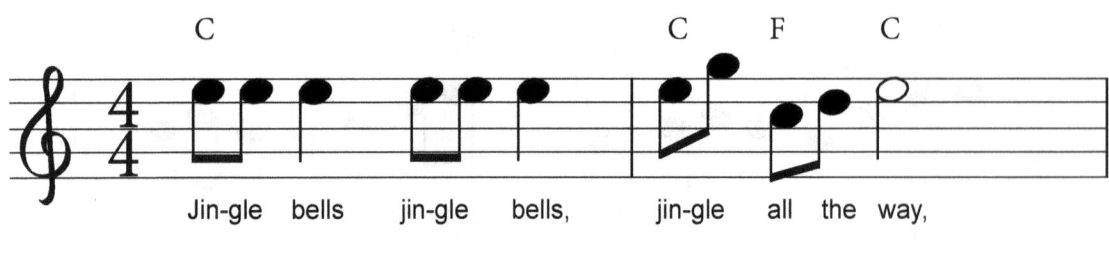

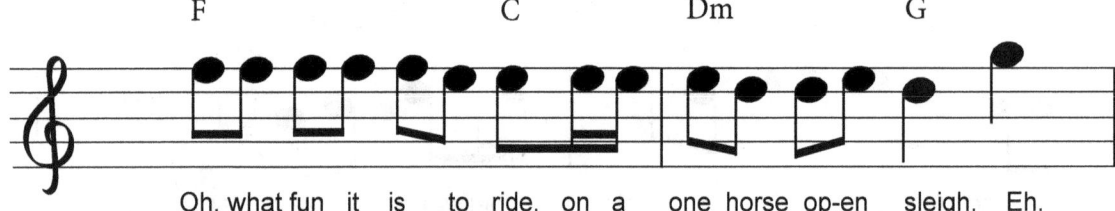

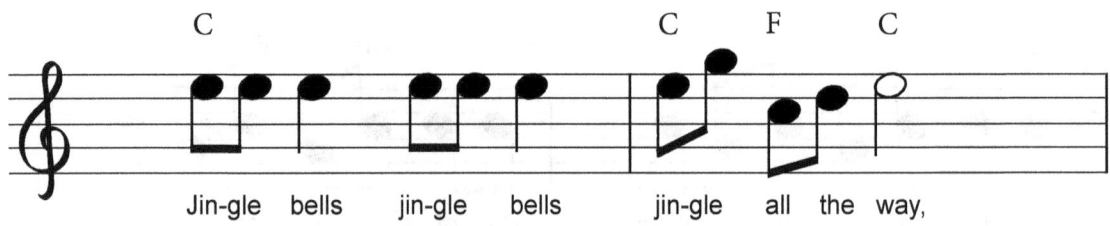

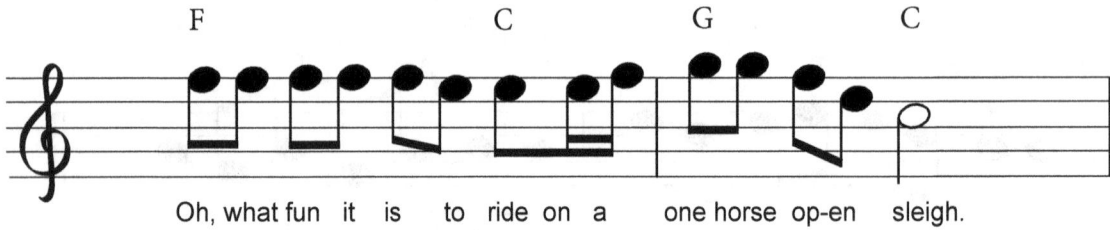

Fig.62

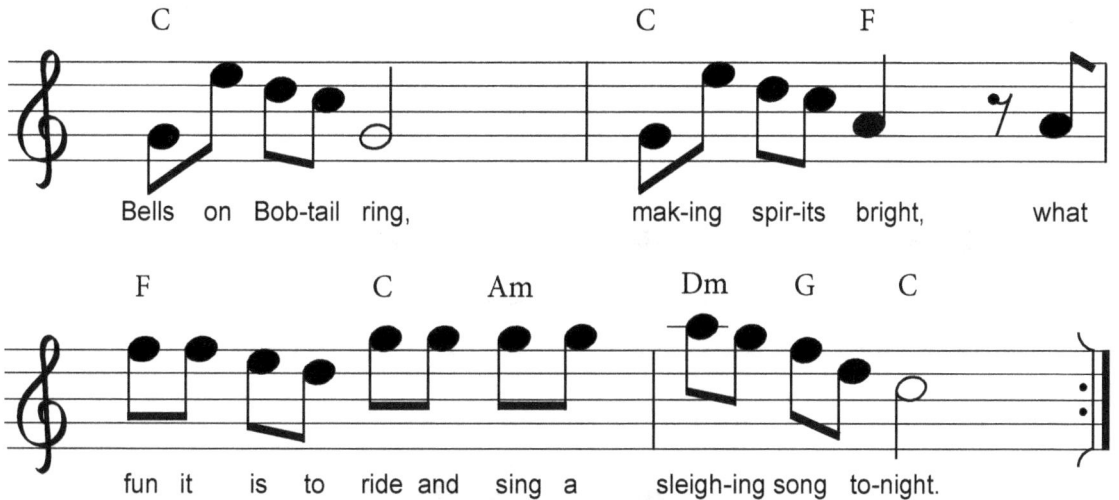

Fig.62 (con't.)

Twinkle Twinkle Little Star

Jane Taylor
1806

Fig.63

Rock-A-Bye Boo

John Sebastian Gaskin
© 2002 BMI

Fig.64

There are compositions with 6/8 time signature, in which there are six eight notes per measure. In some compositions you will not see six eight notes but the values of each measure adds up to six eight notes. When the beat is indicated in 6/8 timing and dotted quarter notes are used then the rhythm has a two beats per measure feel, where three eight notes are included in each beats (Fig.65). Keep the metronome very slow to beat each eight note, feel the beats.

Pop Goes The Weasel

Traditional
1855

♩. = 110   Lively

Fig.65

This is the end of **Guitar-1: Beginning Guitar-Music Theory-Sight Reading.** I hope you have gained much knowledge and training from what was presented here. I hope that you are eager to continue your growth in your guitar playing and music. The second book in the series, **Guitar-2: Intermediate Guitar-Music Theory-Sight Reading**, continues the teachings to help you, the student, grow.

16 - References

Images courtesy of **John Sebastian Gaskin** (except as indicated)

Acoustic Guitar - **Kamouraska Concert 162F**

Electric Guitar - **Ibanez Artist EQ**

Tuners - **Korg CA-30;**
Korg Pitchclip Tuner courtesy Korg.com

Metronomes - **Zen-on Metrina;**
SX Metronome courtesy of edequity.com

Image of John Gaskin courtesy of Clayton Philip

All songs shown are in the public domain, except for '**Then There's Ten**' and '**Rock-A-Bye Boo**' written by **John Sebastian Gaskin**

The guitars shown in this book are guitars that I own.

Recommended Books:

Noad, F. M. (1968). *Solo Guitar Playing. A complete course of instructions in the techniques of guitar performance*. Schirmer Books - A division of Macmillan publishing Co. Inc. New York, N.Y.

Randel, D. M. (1978). *Harvard Concise Dictionary of Music*. Harvard University Press. Belknap Press. Cambridge, Mass.

Starer, R. (1969). *Rhythmic Training*. Universal - MCA Music Publishing Inc. Hal Leonard Publishing. New York, N.Y.

Self-Notes

Self-Notes

John Sebastian Gaskin

John Sebastian Gaskin is a musician, composer and now author. He has performed in New York, New Jersey, Connecticut, Delaware, Philadelphia, Trinidad and Tobago. He has studied music at Brooklyn College, New York. He studied guitar starting with Anthony 'Pimpa' Springer in Trinidad and with Steve Adelson in Brooklyn, New York.

"Special appreciation go out to two guitarists who have encouraged me, guided me, taught me, influenced me; Anthony 'Pimpa' Springer and Wayne B. Bruno."

"I have made mention of Robert Starer earlier in the book. Robert Starer and Noah Creshevsky are two of my music teachers at Brooklyn College, who saw something in me, believed in me and encouraged me to believe in myself and my ability."

Other Book in the Series:
Guitar-2   Intermediate: Guitar - Music Theory - Sight Reading.
Bass-1   Beginning: Bass Guitar - Music Theory - Sight Reading.
Piano-1   Beginning: Piano - Music Theory - Sight Reading.

GUITAR-1
©-2016 Jo-Kin Music - BMI

ISBN: 978-976-95914-2-4

www.ingramcontent.com/pod-product-compliance
Lightning Source LLC
Chambersburg PA
CBHW081328040426
42453CB00013B/2329